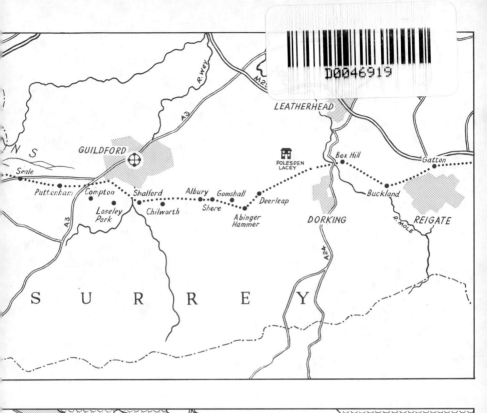

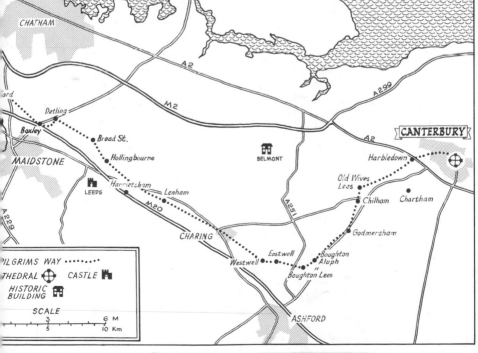

The Road to Canterbury
A Modern Pilgrimage

SHIRLEY DU BOULAY

Illustrated by Ursula Sieger

MOREHOUSE PUBLISHING
Harrisburg, PA

First published in Great Britain in 1994
by HarperCollins*Publishers*

First U.S. edition published in 1995 by:

Morehouse Publishing

Editorial Office:
871 Ethan Allen Hwy.
Ridgefield, CT 06877

Corporate Office:
P.O. Box 1321
Harrisburg, PA 17105

ISBN: 0-8192-1645-3

Library of Congress Cataloging-in-Publication Data

Du Boulay, Shirley.
  The road to Canterbury : a modern pilgrimage / Shirley Du Boulay :
illustrated by Ursula Sieger.
    p. cm.
  Originally published: Great Britain : HarperCollins, 1994.
  Includes bibliographical references and index.
  ISBN 0-8192-1645-3 (pbk.)
  1. Christian pilgrims and pilgrimages—England—Winchester.
2. Christian pilgrims and pilgrimages—England—Canterbury. 3. Du
Boulay, Shirley—Journeys—England. 4. Catholics—England—
Biography. 5. England—Description and travel. I. Title.
  BX2320.5.E54D8   1995   95-22775
  263'.042422—dc20   CIP

Printed in the United States of America

IN MEMORY OF JOHN

Contents

Acknowledgements

My most grateful thanks to my companions Eileen and Jane and our driver Barbara; to all who gave us help and hospitality on the pilgrimage, especially Canon Robert Teare, the Snells, the Meyers, the Gullands, Mrs Atkins and Canon Christopher and Rhona Lewis; to my editor Giles Semper and my agent Jacqueline Korn for their continual support and encouragement; to Valerie Elliston, for the meticulous care with which she compiled the index; to Alex and Clare Eaglestone, Sara Hicks, Deborah Honore, Maureen Taylor and again my companions, who read the manuscript and made helpful suggestions; to all responsible for keeping the Pilgrims' Way open to walkers.

ST CATHERINE'S MAZE

Prologue

I moved slowly and silently, apart from my companion. I was walking the Winchester Mizmaze, an ancient turf labyrinth on St Catherine's Hill. It stretches comfortably across part of the top of the hill, near the site of the chapel, and is roughly square, measuring 86 by 90 feet. I set foot on it apprehensively, wondering what I would experience, wondering whether I would experience anything at all. It is a unicursal maze, in other words there are no choices – just keep going and you must reach the centre. Almost immediately I was filled with a great sense of trust. I knew that this simple track would not mislead me; if I followed it faithfully I would arrive where I wished to be. To and fro, criss-crossing the holy hill, I covered quite a distance and was aware that I was becoming intimately acquainted with the terrain, feeling at home in this intricate weaving. Often, as is the way with the labyrinthine pattern, the path took me away from the centre, but this did not diminish the sense of trust as I went on, almost hypnotic-ally . . .

Then, so suddenly that it was with a sense of shock, I was there, standing in the centre, a rough log my only company. Did I feel any different, having accomplished this small feat? I did. But why? And how? I could not lay claim to any great achievement – it was not far, nor was it hard – but the tortuous path had honoured my trust and led me to the centre. I was filled with a sense of security and wholeness, the one-pointedness of a good meditation. I stood there in thrall, wondering at the effect of so simple an action. Time was suspended. I could hardly tell how long I stayed thus, but it was probably only a matter of minutes. Then some children arrived at the periphery of the maze; at the edge of consciousness I heard them laughing and talking as I remained separate, sealed off in my safe, womb-like little world. Suddenly one of the children, spurning the long winding path, scampered straight across the maze and jumped into my pool of quiet, shouting 'I've won'. I was jerked back into the competitive world.

The Christian tradition has long seen the maze as a symbol of pilgrimage and in the Middle Ages to tread a maze was to make a symbolic pilgrimage to Jerusalem. In a few months' time I would be walking the Pilgrims' Way from Winchester to Canterbury and before I did so I was keen to taste pilgrimage in miniature, as it were taking an aperitif before the main meal. Making this mini-journey around Saint Catherine's Hill endorsed my growing conviction that to make a physical pilgrimage would add a subtle dimension to the inner journey.

But before I donned my walking boots and set out along the banks of the Itchen river there was much to do. First I wanted to learn something about the tradition of the pilgrims in whose footsteps I would be following. I needed to understand something of medieval piety and the way medieval man regarded pilgrimage, relics, saints and martyrs; to know about the practicalities of their journeys – how they travelled, what they wore, how they relaxed, where they slept. I wanted to enter, at every level, into the nature of pilgrimage and to share and understand the passion that animated those who had travelled before.

I also had to get physically fit. The journey is about 130 miles and my companions and I were intending to do it in about twelve days. To a serious walker this is quite a leisurely stroll, but I had not walked any distance for three decades; also I had had three operations in the previous eighteen months. I began to take regular exercise. Bike and car stood idle as I seized every excuse to walk ~ to the shops; to visit friends; to libraries (to read about pilgrimage), to think, to talk. I walked on Oxfordshire towpaths, over muddy fields, on tarmac roads and, when I could find them, up hills. I was resolved to walk every inch of the Pilgrims' Way, banishing any temptation to use modern means of transport. And I was determined to be fit enough to enjoy the walk, leaving my mind free to absorb the experience and to encounter fully whatever might happen along the way.

MEDIEVAL PILGRIM

Chapter One

Questions

'Why do you want to make a pilgrimage?' 'Are you a keen walker?' 'What made you choose the Pilgrims' Way?' These were just some of the questions I was asked as I prepared for the walk from Winchester to Canterbury. I was intrigued by the interest pilgrimage aroused in my friends; by the way they wanted to share their experiences, by their readiness to lend books and pass on information. Many of them wanted to be in some way involved, and after only a few minutes' conversation we were touching on the profound parallels between life and pilgrimage that the subject stimulated. The idea of pilgrimage struck a deep resonance and their questions forced me to examine my own motivation.

The idea of making a pilgrimage had been suggested by a friend some two years after my husband's death; it was one of those moments of illumination that can appear when life is at its bleakest. After months and months of apathy and indifference I was immediately excited, curious, expectant. It was as if a light had been switched on.

I wondered why. I have never been a particularly keen walker – if only because in my childhood to enjoy walking was almost a moral prerequisite – though I was attracted by the thought of the physical activity and the challenge to complete an undertaking. I was drawn to the idea of travelling through beautiful scenery in agreeable company and the deep satisfaction of going slowly, able to feel the earth under my feet, savour my surroundings. But those things could be found in any long-distance walk and there was more to my excitement than that. There was, if I dared admit it, a surging of hope.

My excitement at the thought of making a pilgrimage lay in the symbolism of the journey, the search. When I was about fifteen I had one of those experiences of union, a sense of oneness with nature and with God, that (though I did not realize it at the time) set me on the path of the searcher. Since then I have been pursued by what Francis Thompson called 'The Hound of Heaven' and though I have sometimes blessed him, sometimes wished he would go away, he refuses to give up the chase. Perhaps it was possible, by trudging the long miles from departure to destination, to learn more about the universal pilgrimage, the journey we all make from birth to death. Perhaps this physical re-enactment of the inner search might shed some light on my own doubts and questions, might even heal my own wounds.

I began to understand, more fully than ever before, why pilgrimage has been called 'the poor man's mysticism' and why, since the beginning of time, people have made long, arduous and sometimes dangerous journeys, crossed seas and continents to visit sacred sites. But I was confused about which was the stronger, the mysterious pull of a holy place or the significance of the journey itself. My first instinct was that, for today's pilgrim, the attraction would lie more in the journey than the arrival; in fact I soon realized that they symbolize different aspects of our spiritual need and have to be distinguished.

A desire to stand on holy ground, to be in a place where the veil between heaven and earth has grown thin, seems to be a deep human instinct. I like the way that great scholar of comparative religion Professor Mircea Eliade put it when he wrote that 'every pilgrimage shrine is an archetype of the sacred centre'. In a sacred place we may experience the transcendent, the 'timeless moment', a universal God, above the differences of religion or denomination. It is paradoxical that we should claim that God is everywhere and yet seek him in special places, yet it is a paradox which we, having created, need to accept. I wondered whether we are drawn to holy places because we need to externalize the sacred centre within us all. The thought that God is within us is too frightening; we need to locate him somewhere else. There is also the argument that we may need to find God in a particular place before we can realize that he is everywhere.

And pilgrimage itself can symbolize not only our journey from birth to death but the thread of the inner journey. Everyone must express his own inner journey. It can be a journey from sin to salvation, from confusion to clarity, from resistance to acceptance, from Godlessness to a real perception of God, from God without to God within. What did I hope from it? I was not sure. I wanted to learn to let go, to accept, to love unconditionally, to be rather than to do. But most of all on this pilgrimage I wanted to have an open mind, ready to receive whatever came my way.

Such possibilities! No wonder pilgrimage has drawn mankind down the centuries. No wonder I was filled with such expectant curiosity.

So which pilgrimage should I make? Pilgrimage is enjoying great popularity today and in this country alone there are many to choose from. The classic definition of pilgrimages is that they are 'journeys to holy places undertaken from motives of devotion in order to obtain supernatural help or as acts of penance or thanksgiving',[1] today, however, this is interpreted rather more freely. A recent article[2] divides pilgrimages into those on foot, on cycles, or 'in spirit'. The pilgrimages on foot included 'Island Hopping, Hill Walking and Worshipping in Out-of-the-Way Places' and a diocesan Easter walking pilgrimage to various cathedrals in the south of England. The cyclists were represented by a Yorkshire woman, Rebecca Hodel, who cycled to all the Church of England cathedrals as an act of thanksgiving for the vote on women's ordination and Mrs Phyllis Nye, who, at 70 years old, cycled to the greatest pilgrimage centre of all, Santiago de Compostela. The example of pilgrimages in spirit was a series of lectures organized by the Confraternity of St James, a society organized to bring together people interested in the pilgrimage to Santiago de Compostela.

I wanted to walk, I favoured walking in Great Britain or Ireland and was keen to be anchored in the tradition of the Middle Ages, the Golden Age of pilgrimage. The choice lay between the numerous Irish shrines like Lough Derg, Croagh Patrick or the more recent shrine at Knock; Iona, a sacred place even before the arrival of Saint Columba in the sixth century and a place of pilgrimage since his death; Walsingham, one of the most important centres in medieval England, and Canterbury.

There were many reasons for my choice of Canterbury. For over three hundred years after the murder of Thomas Becket in 1170 his shrine was one of the most popular in the whole of Europe. What better route could I take if I wanted to share the experience of the medieval pilgrims? Further, the story is one of the best known in British history; it has been immortalized in Chaucer's *Canterbury Tales* and T. S. Eliot's *Murder in the Cathedral*, and the pilgrimage has left its legacy in everyday language – 'Canterbury Bells' from the bells worn on pilgrims' horses, the word 'canter', from the 'Canterbury-gallop' (the easy pace with which they moved), even the word 'Canterbury' is sometimes used as an epithet for a long and tedious story.

Further I knew that much of the route lay along the North Downs Way and was very beautiful; I was stirred by its importance in English history as the Saxon capital of Kent whose King, Ethelbert, welcomed Augustine's mission from Rome. It is also a pilgrimage that not only has an end, but a beginning, for though Chaucer's pilgrims travelled from London, there is also a route from Winchester to Canterbury traditionally taken by the pilgrims. Though this has been argued, even dismissed as romantic fantasy, there is a strong case in its favour, strong enough to ensure that this route is inscribed in memory, even marked on modern maps as 'The Pilgrims' Way'.

I became a Roman Catholic in 1989, but am too late a convert for relationships with saints and the reverence of relics and shrines to come naturally and cannot claim to have chosen this route out of a particular devotion to Saint Thomas Becket; I was drawn more by the thought of those who had walked before. The idea that this could have been the route taken by the medieval pilgrims appealed to me; but even if it were proved to be fantasy, I could take comfort in the fact that there is no doubt that the Pilgrims' Way from Winchester to Canterbury is an ancient way, used by mankind for thousands of years. However changed it might now be, I would be following the footsteps of men, women and animals who had trodden the same path, sharing the experience of pagans and Christians, of Neolithic man and twentieth-century backpackers. It was above all this primal, atavistic, aspect to the Pilgrims' Way that excited me.

But pilgrimage concerns the body as much as the mind and spirit, it bridges the concrete reality of physical life and the elusive abstraction of the holy. So I should not have been so surprised by the curiosity my friends showed about the practicalities involved in a long walk. On my return I was greeted by such questions as 'Did you go alone?' 'What did you wear?' 'What did you do about luggage?' 'Where did you stay?' 'How many miles did you walk every day?' 'Did you plan it all beforehand – where you would stay and where you would eat?' 'How long did it take?' It seems fitting to answer some of these eager questions.

So – Did I go alone? I had considered it, feeling that there would be greater freedom to follow my own whims, take my own pace, think my own thoughts. Also I was worried that, not being in top physical condition, I might become a burden to anyone accompanying me. But though I need and enjoy solitude in small doses, I knew that over a long period I would have become bored and lonely, yearning to talk and to share experiences, jokes, a bottle of wine. Also I was constantly reminded that nowadays there are risks for a woman walking alone and, though I was put to shame by hearing of solitary adventures undertaken by braver women than I, I had no wish to walk in fear. For the medieval pilgrim there were many threats ~ bandits, thieves, and wild beasts. We did not need to fear wild beasts, but thieves and bandits have their modern equivalents.

So I was delighted to find others keen to come and willing to spare the time. As my companions wish to remain in misty anonymity I shall simply say that one, Jane, was a very close friend I have known for over thirty years and who lives abroad at present. Eileen is an Oxford friend and though we have not known each other for long she became very involved with the whole venture, helping to plan the route and braving wind and weather as we took regular exercise together. The third, Barbara, did not want to walk, but preferred to drive, spending the day painting and drawing along the route and meeting us in the evenings. So we were three walkers, four for friendly evenings and meals; it was a good balance.

The wish of one of our number to drive also solved another problem ~ what did we do with our luggage? Of course there are the doughty hikers who travel with all their needs on their backs, but it was unrealistic to think that three middle-aged women could do that. On the way we heard of various ways in which other walkers, unwilling or unable to be so burdened, cope with this problem. There are those who drive to the day's goal, take public transport back to the departure point and then walk to their vehicle. Then there are some who leave their baggage at their night's lodging and trust a taxi to take it to the next stopover; others who use their own car, paying a local driver to take it and its contents to an agreed meeting place. We, blessed with our voluntary artist/driver, were spared these complicated and expensive options. Our luggage stayed in Barbara's car and we met up with her and it in the evenings.

The use of a car and a driver also solved another problem, how to reach our night's lodgings without adding tiring miles to our day's travel. As we were planning to complete the journey in about twelve days, we needed to average thirteen miles a day. (Though the Pilgrims' Way is said to be about 130 miles, allowing for diversions for lunches and visiting sites just off the route, not to mention the occasions when we got lost, we covered at least 150 miles.) The other side of the pleasure of walking mostly in woods, over fields and downs, by river banks, was that it was seldom possible to find bed and breakfast accommodation - which in any case had to be booked in advance - without diverting from our route. Three or four miles more is three miles or four miles too much at the end of a long day's walk, but it is nothing by car, so we shamelessly asked Barbara to pick us up and drive us to wherever we were staying. I say shamelessly, but we were also scrupulous. If not marking our last steps with chalk, at least the next morning we would go back to exactly the point where we had left off the night before.

In all these practical matters the medieval pilgrims were never far from my thoughts; what would their answers to these questions have been? Less pressurized by time than their twentieth-century successors they spent at least four weeks walking from Winchester to Canterbury. They would not have had to plan their day's travel or make long detours to find bed and board; in those days hospices, inns and monasteries could be found along the route and they would simply have stopped when they were tired. While it is no longer possible to ride along the Pilgrims' Way, they could, and some who could afford it did, travel by coach or on horseback. Many more went on foot.

There were constant reminders of how different the landscape would have been, how different from us they would have looked. While we, wearing trousers and anoraks, rucksacks on our backs, guidebook in hand, were indistinguishable from other walkers, the pilgrim of the Middle Ages demonstrated his new, if normally temporary, way of life in wearing what was virtually a uniform, a declaration of his special status. He would have worn a sclavein, a long, coarse, russet-coloured tunic with large sleeves, occasionally patched with crosses. A leather belt was suspended round his shoulders and from it hung a soft pouch known as a scrip in which he would keep his money. A rosary of large beads would hang from his neck or arm and, most distinctively of all, he would carry a staff, a tough wooden stick with a metal toe, and wear a large, broad-brimmed hat, attached at the back to a long scarf. The hat might be decorated with scallop shells or with small lead images of the Mother of God and the saints. As the old ballad about the girl seeking her lover reminds us he, on pilgrimage and clothed in 'pilgrim's weedes', would have been easily recognizable.

> And how should I your true love know
> From many another one?
> O by his cockle hat and staff
> And by his sandal shoone.

As with so many objects of medieval times, the pilgrim's apparel was invested with an elaborate symbolism. The pouch was usually small, too small to hold much money and thus showing the pilgrim's dependence on charity. The staff was used to fend off wolves and wild dogs, who represented the snares of the devil, but also for support, thus becoming the pilgrim's third leg and symbolic of the Trinity. Put the two symbols together and staff and wild beasts come to represent the conflict between the Trinity and the forces of evil. Sometimes the tunic, not unlike the garments Christ might have worn, represented his humanity. And the wood of the staff, in recalling the wood of the Cross, reminded the pilgrim of his hope of salvation.

Once into a symbolic way of thinking every aspect of pilgrimage becomes charged with new meaning. For instance a fifteenth-century Dominican broadened the significance of the staff, pouch and tunic by suggesting that they represented faith, hope and charity. So too does this imagery often find poetic expression, most famously in Sir Walter Ralegh's poem.

> Give me my scallop shell of quiet
>   My staff of faith to walk upon;
> My scrip of joy, immortal diet;
>   My bottle of salvation;
> My gown of glory, hopes true gage,
> And thus I'll take my pilgrimage.[3]

Nor should we forget the rest of the poem, in which Ralegh's soul travelled 'towards the land of heaven' where 'it will thirst no more'.

Less familiar is a fourteenth-century French treatise called the *Pèlerinage de la Vie Humaine*. The Cistercian author recalls a dream in which he undertakes a pilgrimage to the celestial Jerusalem.

> Dame Grace blesses him and offers him the scarf of faith and the stave of hope. On the road he is attacked by the deadly sins in the form of wild beasts. Heresy, voluptuousness, and idleness lie in wait to attack and rob him. He is shipwrecked in the sea of worldliness and is near to drowning when he succeeds in saving himself by climbing onto the raft of the Cistercian order.[4]

Though symbolic thinking does not come instinctively to the modern mind as it did to the medieval, indeed can sometimes appear naïve, I found I was envious of the significance with which everything connected with pilgrimage used to be imbued; wistful that, apart perhaps from some very personal possessions, everything we wore or carried revealed our concern with the practical and the prosaic rather than the poetic. It would have been an affectation to try to transfer the old symbolism directly to our accoutrements, but symbolic interpretations kept striking me. For instance our dependence on our guidebook, without which we could have got lost or have found ourselves on dangerous motorways. We did not use a compass, but there were at least three occasions when its skilful use would have saved us taking a wrong direction; for us, as for the nineteenth-century poet Thomas Moore, it could have been a reminder that 'the needle points faithfully o'er the dim sea'. Then there was our gratitude for strong, sturdy and comfortable boots, recalling the importance of firm foundations. Our light, warm clothes, adapting so easily to the changing weather, could be seen as symbols of flexibility, essential to every pilgrim. And what is the spiritual equivalent of the Ordnance Survey Map? I think it is not too fanciful to suggest that it might lie in the writings of people like St Teresa of Avila, who charted the inner journey with as much care as any cartographer mapping more tangible terrain. Most of all, something that struck me every day, was the importance of travelling light.

All these things were to flick across the landscape of my mind as we walked, but none more than that first question ~ Did you walk alone? It was to stand at the centre of the tension between the joys of companionship and the peace of solitude; it was to appear in relationship to freedom, to selfishness and giving, to pace, continuity and rhythm, to the experience of being 'Alone with the Alone'. Seen from a medieval perspective, it had to do with virtue, with the merit to be derived from pilgrimage, for though in those days few did travel alone, to do so was thought to be especially virtuous.

Why it should have been so raises a hornet's nest of questions. Solitude brought risks, there was no question about that. Travelling in those days was a dangerous business and, despite the special protection given to pilgrims, their regular passing was too great a temptation to the professional robber bands, villagers and innkeepers, who constantly chanced their luck and flouted the law. Murders, especially on the hazardous routes to Jerusalem and Rome, were commonplace. Jonathan Sumption notes that in 1350 no less than half the pilgrims who set out for Rome were robbed or killed. He also tells of an innkeeper in the forest of Châtenay, near Mâcon, who used to give travellers a bed for the night and murder them as they slept. An investigation into these tales revealed eighty-eight hidden bodies.[5]

So the pilgrim who walked alone must receive high marks for courage. So too, unable to seek cover in the warmth and laughter of companionship, he would have had more time and space to face the demons in his heart. But the desire for company is a natural human instinct and there are rewards to be won in learning to live with others, in enduring the irritations that are part of relationship, in *not* having room to follow every impulse, muse without interruption, in learning to be quiet with God while surrounded by people. The pleasures of company and community are deep in the pilgrimage ideal, indeed I know a Benedictine monk who joined the order as a direct result of the spirit of community he found on a pilgrimage in Scotland. It seems that, in the matter of solitude, it is more a question of different, rather than better, ways to grow and improve, just as the celibate and the married state offer different ways to holiness.

For the medieval mind, to suffer, even to the point of masochism, was one of the ways to speed the climb to heaven. So the merits of the journey were judged in direct relationship to the pain and incovenience endured. Thus it was thought better to go on foot than on horseback, better still to go alone on foot, even better not to wear shoes at all. There are even recorded cases when an exceptionally ascetic, extravagantly humble pilgrim (though even in the middle ages they were rare) would arrive at the shrine alone, barefoot and stark naked.

My attitude would not have earned me high marks. I verge towards hedonism rather than masochism and, apart from my almost fanatical wish to walk every inch of the way, I saw no reason not to be as comfortable as possible ~ and that included walking with friends. I suspect in this I was a fairly typical child of my time.

Another question I was sometimes asked was whether we prayed together. Two of us were Roman Catholics, one an Anglican and one calls herself a lapsed Catholic, but there was far more that united us than divided us, and we had no problem in finding a way to come together most evenings and sit quietly for a while. We had intended to discuss thoughts that had come to us during the day, but when the time came we were usually too tired, sometimes too occupied with the practicalities of the journey. So usually we would meditate in silence for a while, then one of us would read a prayer or a poem. One of my favourites was written by the great seventeenth-century Indian poet Tukuram:

Wheresoever I go, Thou art my companion:
Thou takest me by the hand and guidest me.
As I walk along I lean on Thee,
And thou goest with me carrying my burden.
If in my distress I speak frantically,
Thou commandest my words, and thus
Takest away my shame, and I am made bold.
Now I know that every man is a friend dear to me.
I pray, says Tura, with childish delight:
For I feel Thy bliss within and without me.[6]

THE RIVER ITCHEN

Chapter Two

Winchester to Ropley

The first step

By the time the moment came, 3 May had arrived, and we were set to start, my excitement had turned to panic. I couldn't understand it. I was only going for a fortnight's walk, in gentle English countryside with three good friends, yet I was in a state only a few shakes away from terror.

Perhaps it was not totally inappropriate. The unexpected is part and parcel of travel and if to make a pilgrimage is to mirror life in microcosm, then it is fitting to embark on it with a degree of apprehension. It wasn't that I expected anything dreadful to happen outwardly, my anxiety was more over what I would experience inwardly. Would I encounter depths in which I would rather not swim, meet buried emotions I would rather not unearth? I found I was fantasizing about other sorts of journeys, wondering, for instance, if the unborn child unknowingly experiences such fears before erupting from the womb and into life. Then there was the fear that I would experience nothing at all, and the thought of that blank emptiness was even worse. There was no pleasing me. On the one hand all I wanted to do was to curl up in bed, hidden deep in warmth, on the other I knew that I would feel deeply disappointed – and deeply ashamed – if I turned back before I had even started.

I had been consoled by the words of a wise friend, who had written to me saying, 'Just give yourself to the pilgrimage and don't think about anything except what's going on from moment to moment.' Yet the night before, reading Belloc's *The*

Path to Rome, the peace arising from my resolution to live in the present was disturbed again. The phrase that set Belloc writing was '*Ce n'est que le premier pas qui coute*' - 'It is only the first step that counts'. He finds it false, but admits that 'It is just true enough to remain fast in the mind'. Certainly it haunted me. If it is only the first step that counts, what a world would be invested in that step. In any case when would it be taken, when does a pilgrimage begin? I imagined myself pinioned to the ground outside Winchester Cathedral, too fearful of the implications of that first step to move, looking longingly backwards at the life I was temporarily leaving behind and, like Lot's wife, turned into a pillar of salt, a new curiosity for passers-by. I decided to forget the French proverb-maker and remember the wise words of my friend.

Our journey was to start from the cathedral itself, but first, following the tradition of the medieval pilgrims, we went to St John's, the oldest surviving parish church in Winchester. Here the vicar, Canon Robert Teare, read a short and ancient service, the *Itinerarium for Pilgrims*. He invoked the blessing of the Archangel Raphael - one of the seven archangels who stands continually in the presence of God - then read the Benedictus and a few prayers. He prayed for God's protection, for:

> a support in setting out, a solace on the way, a shadow in the heat, a cover from the rain and cold, a chariot in weariness, a protection in danger, a staff in slippery places, a harbour in shipwreck, that under your guidance they may happily reach the place whither they are going, and at length return to their homes in safety.

I was particularly touched by this passage (though on this countryside route there did not seem to be much likelihood that we would be shipwrecked), but I did wonder about the 'chariot in weariness'. What of my resolve to walk the whole way, whatever the temptations to accept a lift? It was reassuring to feel that this traditional prayer would allow me to give in to exhaustion, though I was not convinced that this was part of the bargain I had made with myself.

I was also interested that the *Itinerarium* makes no mention of confession or absolution. The medieval pilgrim would, before his departure, seek the permission of his wife, his parish priest and his feudal lord; he would make his will, set his affairs in order and – most importantly – make amends to anyone he had wronged. He would probably have attended Mass, then, at either a public or private ceremony, he would receive a formal blessing (such as the *Itinerarium*) in which his clothes, his wallet and mantle, his emblems, rucksack and staff, would also be blessed. Thus he was initiated, in a sense becoming a member of an 'order' of the church, with the special status and privileges that were the right of the true pilgrim. If he then made his confession – and it does not seem to have been obligatory – his penance, the expiation of his sins, lay in the pilgrimage itself.

When the short service was over, Canon Teare showed us the 'squints' close to the altar, through which the medieval pilgrims would have seen Mass being celebrated, and Beggar's Lane, to the north of the church, so called as the beggars used to collect there, hoping to take advantage of the pious state of the pilgrims as they started out on their journey. Then we modern pilgrims, blessed in this ancient tradition, walked to the cathedral as Canon Teare regaled us with some of the less familiar facts about Winchester. He told us that in the Middle Ages there were 55 parish churches within the city walls; that the grounds of Winchester College boast the longest avenue of Siberian Wing-nuts in the world; that the grass within the Bishop's Palace is the only piece of lawn in the city not fouled by dogs; that the large and imposing house, Number One, The Close, was once the home of Mary Sumner, founder of the Mother's Union. Having just left the vicarage at Old

Alresford, so large that it is now the diocesan retreat house, she complained that her new Winchester mansion was too small.

To travel from Winchester to Canterbury is to travel between two ancient cities with long and eventful histories. Settlements on both sites date from prehistoric times; great Roman roads radiate from both; an eighth-century map of England shows few other towns in the southeast of England and none between Winchester and Canterbury. So what of Winchester, the city from which this first step was to be taken?

My only personal connection with the city is that one of the houses of Winchester College was founded in 1862 by the Reverend James du Boulay, a schoolmaster who was I believe a first cousin twice removed. I knew that for many years it had been known as 'Cook's', so when I went to see it I was amazed to find DU BOULAY'S, my own maiden name, emblazoned on its stone walls. It gave me a warm sense of belonging.

Today Winchester, like most modern cities, is not a place for driving; enclosed in a car I have found myself pulled in confused circles round one-way streets, anger mounting as I lost all sense of direction in a maze of modern roads and buildings, reaching a paroxysm of despair as, just to the north, one sees the great scar of the new road built over Twyford Down. On the other hand to wander on foot round the streets is to find that it is still a beautiful city, filled with the ghosts from centuries of English history – the Celts for whom it was Caer Gwent, 'the white town'; Roman soldiers walking the long roads they built connecting the city with Southampton, Dorchester, Cirencester and Silchester; Saxons who, tempted by Winchester's position at the centre of this network, challenged and conquered. Under them the city became the capital of Wessex and when the kings of Wessex became kings of all England the city for a time rivalled the capital itself. The Danish invasion brought King Canute, most vividly remembered for deflating his flattering courtiers by showing them that the sea would not retreat at his command.

One of Winchester's most prized possessions is the Round Table of King Arthur, which has hung in the Great Hall of Winchester Castle since it was built there at the end of the thirteenth century. It is made from 121 separate pieces of oak, it measures 18 feet across and weighs well over a ton. In 1522 King Henry VIII proudly took the Emperor Charles V to see it, claiming it was one of the most interesting sights in the kingdom. Henry had had it painted in the Tudor colours of green and white, with the Tudor Rose in the centre and a picture of King Arthur at the top, the names of 24 of his favourite knights round the edge. (The table's circular shape was to ensure that there were no arguments about precedence among the knights.) No doubt Henry's pride owed something to the fact that the figure of Arthur bears an extraordinary likeness to the Tudor king himself.

There is a legend that the original table was made by the magician Merlin and seated 150 knights, whose chief pursuit was another kind of pilgrimage – the quest for the Holy Grail. The origins of this legend are obscure. The Grail itself is usually identified with the vessel into which the blood of Christ fell at the Descent from the Cross, but as well as being a Christian symbol of redemption and eternal life it was also a Celtic symbol of plenty. Both legends share the symbolic shedding of light on man's search for value and meaning in life. Both are about journeying.

Once in the cathedral we visited the catafalque of one of Winchester's most famous citizens, St Swithun, the saintly bishop believed to have been tutor to the great King Alfred. Many legends surround this humble and good man. I was charmed to learn that he so disliked the cheers with which he was greeted as he walked around the streets that he took to travelling by night. Another story tells of how he once saw a poor woman drop and break all the eggs she was carrying home. The bishop, concerned at her distress, restored the eggs, miraculously whole, to the basket. By popular consent rather than Roman decree he had already, during his lifetime, come to be regarded as a saint, but the most famous legend associated with him arose after his death. The story is that when he was dying, his humility led him to ask to be buried in the common graveyard 'under the feet of passers-by and rains from the eaves'. A hundred years later, on July 15th, when his body was moved from its modest grave to a shrine within the cathedral, there was a downpour, and it continued for forty days. Were these showers the tears of the saint, dismayed at being moved from the lowly grave of his choice? Thus began the legend concerning his effect on the weather – that if it rains on 15 July, St Swithun's Day, it will rain for forty days; if it is fine on that day it will be fine for forty days.

For two hundred years after his death, until he was superseded by Thomas Becket, his shrine was the object of the most popular pilgrimage in England and, though he is best known for his effect on the weather, he has also left more lasting memorials. He not only built the bridge at the East Gate of the city and enlarged the cathedral, but was co-signatory to the legislation that set aside tithes, in the shape of a tenth of all yearly profits, for the upkeep of the Church.

Having paid homage to Saint Swithun, I lit a candle for John, my husband. I don't understand what it is about lighting candles, but somehow that ephemeral light carries a deep symbolism and it was something I felt compelled to do. Then we were engulfed in another sort of light as we went down to the west door and were greeted by sixteen banners representing the Creation, splendid wings of colour floating down the length of the nave. They are the work of that great religious artist Thetis Blacker, and though I was very familiar with her work and though they are displayed regularly in the cathedral, I had never before seen them all together, or in that magnificent setting. She would, no doubt, have been pleased at the reaction of a young man beside me. 'Wow!' he said, 'Wild!'

Blessed, touched by symbols of healing, love and creation

~ surely these were auspicious conditions in which to take that first step? Yet as we set off on that May morning, the weather as muted and grey as the quiet Bank Holiday streets, I felt irritable and nervous. If it was only the first step that counted, then I was not doing well. As we crossed the pedestrian section of the High Street I was amused to see a white upright piano, sitting at it a young man playing Chopin. I felt I had strayed inadvertently into a surrealist painting and my mood temporarily lightened, only to darken once more as we passed all that remains of the twelfth-century Hyde Abbey, dissolved, stripped and wrecked in 1538 by Henry VIII's commissioner, Thomas Wriothesley. Wriothesley not only took the gold from the shrine to Saint Josse, the lead from the roofs and much of the stone, some of which went towards building himself a house, but then had the temerity and hypocrisy to tell his king, 'We intend to sweep away all the rotten bones that be called relics; which we may not omit, lest it be thought that we came more for the treasure than for the avoiding of the abomination of idolatry.'[1]

Some of the stone Wriothesley did not need for his Winchester house was used for the tower of the adjacent parish church of St Bartholomew, where a stone was found, inscribed 'Alfred Rex DCCCLXXXI', suggesting that King Alfred had been buried there. The stone was stolen many years ago and nothing now remains of the tomb of the great king who made Winchester a seat of learning and who himself translated Bede's *Ecclesiastical History of the English People* and Boethius' *Consolation of Philosophy*; who inspired the compilation of the national year-by-year record known as the *Anglo-Saxon Chronicles*.

As we looked sadly at the ruins of Hyde Abbey we were faced with the first of many decisions about which route to take. It can be argued that the medieval pilgrims would have continued north to Headbourne Worthy. In favour of this choice is the fact that it was a fragment of the Roman road to Silchester and would have been known to the pilgrims coming from the north into Winchester to visit the shrine of St Swithun. Even more telling is the village's Saxon church, dedicated to St Swithun and famous for its great rood of the crucified Christ above the west door. Just as the pilgrims to the shrine of St Swithun must have prayed before it as they neared the end of their journey, so too might the pilgrims to Thomas Becket's shrine have drawn inspiration as they started on their long trek.

The argument for the alternative riverside route is that it is close to water and yet, at least in summer, dry. Also it is the more direct. There can rarely be certainty over the exact path trodden by the pilgrims, or that they all used the same route. We, drawn by the river, chose to take this first opportunity to follow its winding ways.

We were rewarded for this choice by meeting some friends, who live in an idyllic cottage by the river, waiting to greet us as we passed their home. This kindly gesture somehow gave another dimension of meaning to our walk and, feeling slightly like a royal procession, we joined the route from Headbourne Worthy at Kingsworthy Church, where we couldn't resist telling a man tending the churchyard of our destination and were gratified at his admiring response. 'Canterbury? Rather you than me.' Here the ancient track passes the first post office in Britain, becoming a modern high road, so we followed the way suggested by our guidebook[2] and were soon on a narrow path, walking through cow parsley and comfrey along the banks of the Itchen. We passed a huge patch of wild onions, remembering, as we sampled them, that they were a regular part of the diet of our medieval predecessors. Already we were deep in history; indeed Hilaire Belloc, that romantic chronicler of the Pilgrims' Way, observed that here

We were walking these few miles upon earth beaten (to quote recorded history alone) by the flight of Saxons from the battle of Alton, and by the conquering march of Swegen which was the preliminary to the rule of the Danes over England. [3]

Soon our peaceful walking was disrupted by the need to negotiate the A33. I had been revelling in the quiet, yet on this first day was surprised to find that my reaction when we came to a busy road was ambivalent, initial resentment at the intrusion of noise and speed being swiftly followed by a feeling of reassurance that life was streaming on and that help was at hand if needed. (This ambivalence was short-lived; after a day or two, as I became accustomed to the quiet, indeed as it became the norm, quiet was all that I wanted.) The next few miles were pure delight and though I was feeling more like a Bank Holiday walker than a pilgrim, my mood was softened by the beauty surrounding us. The river was full, meandering, gentle in the ease with which it finds its path through the luxuriant vegetation. It reminded me of a passage in the Chinese book of wisdom, the I Ching. Water, the author writes, sets the example for right conduct:

> It flows on and on, and merely fills up all the places through which it flows; it does not shrink from any dangerous spot nor from any plunge, and nothing can make it lose its own essential nature. It remains true to itself under all conditions. Thus likewise, if one is sincere when confronted with difficulties, the heart can penetrate the meaning of the situation. [4]

Far as I was from such wisdom I found that the Itchen is a contented river and that it breeds content, even in irritable walkers. I wished I had brought field glasses, for I had read that its chalky waters attract a miscellany of wild life. I saw trout, coots, moorhen and the eternally elegant swans drifting along its surface; I heard blackbirds, thrushes and warblers but did not know how to identify the long-eared, short-eared and pipistrelle bats that can, I was assured, be seen there.

The water meadows bordering the Itchen river are famous for their fertility, the river perplexing in its divisions and meanderings. But doubts about which is the main stream, which the tributary, even the distraction of the constant hum of the M3 and the A33, took second place to sheer delight that, in this stretch at least, the countryside bears some resemblance to the road walked by the poet Edward Thomas in the England before the First World War:

That road, in its winding course from Winchester to Canterbury, through Hampshire, Surrey and Kent, sums up the qualities of roads except those of the straight highway. It is a cart-way from farm to farm; or a foot-path only, or a sheaf of half a dozen footpaths worn side by side; or, no longer needed except by the curious, it is buried under nettle and burdock and barricaded by thorns and traveller's joy and bryony bines; it has been converted into a white country road for a few miles of its length, until an ascent over the Downs or a descent into a valley has to be made, and then once more it is left to footsteps upon grass and bird's foot trefoil or to rude wheels over flints. Sometimes it is hidden among untended hazels or among chalk banks topped with beech and yew, and the kestrel plucks the chaffinch there undisturbed. Or it goes free and hedgeless, like a long balcony half-way up the Downs, and unespied it beholds half the South Country between ash tree boles. Church and inn and farm and cottage and tramp's fire it passes like a wandering wraith of a road.[5]

It was too much to hope that, some eighty years later, nature would be allowed such freedom along the whole Way. We would enjoy it while we could.

The Way passes close to two more 'Worthies' - Abbots Worthy and Martyr Worthy. Worthy is derived from the Saxon 'wordie' - a place or hamlet, but while Abbots Worthy was once the property of an abbot and Kings Worthy that of the Crown, the logic does not extend to Martyr Worthy. It was not a site of martyrdom, but belonged, in the thirteenth century, to the Norman Henricus de la Martre, whose name is derived from the Old French name for a weasel. There are still sheep, a reminder that once the villagers' prosperity was measured by the number of sheep they owned, indeed within living memory an old shepherd, explaining why a farmer had failed, simply said 'The sheep left him.' The village flock was cared for by the church wardens, whose vestments were made from the wool; it was the sheep, not the parishioners, who were referred to as the 'parish flock'. Wool was shipped to Venice and Genoa and in the seventeenth century the industry brought the area even more prosperity, for, in order to encourage the wool trade, an Act of Parliament declared that shrouds must only be made of wool or fine plaid. He who dared bury a relative in any other cloth was compelled to pay a fine.

When we reached Martyr Worthy Church we chatted briefly with the verger, sitting quietly in the sun after cleaning the church, and passed the village hall, proudly displaying a sign offering *The Pirates of Penzance* the following week, and continued along fields and through Chilland to our first stop, Itchen Abbas.

We arrived in time to meet some friends at The Trout for an early lunch. I was still prickly with nerves and cannot have been good company, but we tackled two huge plates of sandwiches, drank bitter shandy (which was to become my favourite pilgrimage drink) and chatted for an hour in this pub (then called The Plough) made famous by Charles Kingsley, who stayed here in 1862 while he was writing the final chapters of *The Water Babies*.

Itchen Abbas is one of many villages along the Pilgrims' Way where there is still tangible proof of the generations that lived and died there. The discovery of flint arrowheads suggest the presence of Neolithic man; chalk coffins found in a vault under the church indicate that the site had religious significance before the stone building was built in the eleventh century; it was the site of a Roman villa and of the Benedictine Abbey of Nunnaminster, founded by the wife of King Alfred the Great and in 1349 devastated, as was much of Hampshire, by the Black Death. Five hundred years later Earl Grey, the Liberal Foreign Secretary, remembered more for his tea than his politics, had a home here, where he used to entertain the famous naturalist W. H. Hudson.

But for me the spirit of this ancient place comes even more vividly to life in a legend. On moonlit nights a headless woman is said to walk up and down the avenue of trees leading to the seventeenth-century rectory. And this, the locals affirm, cannot have been just fancy, for one night in the nineteenth century she was seen clearly by Peter Bignell, the village carpenter, 'a big, burly man with a grey beard, unlikely to tell untruths'.

From Itchen Abbas the Pilgrims' Way would have continued along the high road to Itchen Stoke, so once again we took avoiding action, crossing the river by the church, passing Avington House, owned for a while by King Charles II, who brought Nell Gwyn to stay here when the prebendary of Winchester Cathedral 'refused to give poor Nelly a lodging', and met the old road again at Ovington. There was a deep ford ahead and for a moment I hoped that crossing it might present a challenge and earn us pilgrim status, but a footbridge rendered it distressingly easy, and, slightly deflated, we came to the first of many watercress beds that give yet another use to the waters of the Itchen.

Watercress is unique in that it is a crop grown in running water and in Victorian times farms were established where springs emerged through faults in the clay, releasing pure, relatively warm water from the deep layers of chalk beneath. Each bed contains some six million plants and when all the sowing, transplanting, picking and bunching was done by hand it must have been one of the coldest and wettest of jobs. Now rice planting machines have been adapted to Western use and electric pumps raise the half a million gallons of water needed every day for each acre. This local crop provides nearly a third of the watercress consumed in this country, and has given its name to the 'Watercress Line', ten miles of track from Alresford to Alton, which runs parallel to the Pilgrims' Way and where it is still possible to travel on some of the few remaining steam trains in the country. Indeed I had been advised to take the Watercress Line for part of the walk, but was convinced that this would have been cheating.

Soon we were on Tichborne Down, less than a mile from Tichborne village. So far it had been easy walking, but I had not yet found a rhythm and was beginning to tire. There is no reason to believe that the pilgrims would have strayed from their course to visit Tichborne, and nor did we, but the stories associated with it cannot be left untold.

The Tichborne family have lived in the village since the twelfth century and though during the Reformation they were persecuted and many killed (notably Chidiock Tichborne, excecuted for his part in the Babington Plot against Elizabeth I), they are one of the few families to have remained continuously faithful to the Roman Catholic Church. Tichborne House has its own chapel, but the family also had the use of the parish church, a rare example of an Anglican church in which a part, the north aisle, is officially allowed to be used as a Roman Catholic chapel.

One spring I was visiting a friend who lives in Tichborne, when she showed me a great bag of flour she had just been given and told me the legend of the Tichborne Dole. Lady Mabella, wife of Sir Roger Tichborne, was dying. As her last wish she asked her husband to allow her the money to leave a bequest granting flour to all who should come to the house asking for it on 25 March, Lady Day. His callous response was to offer corn from all the land round which she could walk in the time that it took a blazing brand to burn. Too ill to walk, she somehow managed to crawl round twenty-three acres. The field is still called The Crawls and the dole ~ six pounds of flour for every adult, three for every child ~ is still distributed every March by the head of the Tichborne family.

But this tale born of charity and cruelty does not end here. Lady Mabella had laid a curse on any Tichborne who failed to distribute the dole; should this happen the next generation would consist of seven daughters, the family would die out and the house would fall down. In 1796 the dole was not distributed, in 1803 part of the house fell down and the successor to the baronetcy produced seven daughters and no son. So the huge estates came to a nephew, another Roger Tichborne, and thus to the tale of the Tichborne Claimant.

In 1854, when Roger Tichborne was only 25, he was thought to have been drowned at sea, though his mother, refusing to believe it, advertised widely, offering a reward to anyone who could find her beloved son. Eventually a large, middle-aged man claimed his inheritance. Though he was recognized by his mother as her son and was supported by some of the locals, the rest of the family declared him an impostor. A great deal of money was at stake and the affair caused an international sensation; there was a civil law suit lasting 103 days, followed in 1871 by a criminal action lasting ten months (the longest trial ever held in this country) in which the Tichborne Claimant was tried for perjury. He was found guilty and sentenced to fourteen years penal servitude. The controversy did not end and the truth will probably never now be known.

The Itchen had now left us, turning south at Tichborne to find its source near New Cheriton, the day was close and warm and the last few miles of this first day's walk, through Bishops Sutton to Ropley Dean, though pleasant enough, was an anticlimax after the beauty of the river bank. My irritability and nervousness had gone, but the new demon, as I only realize fully with hindsight, was the various physical afflictions, ranging from discomfort to excruciating pain, that had begun. I came to regard these aches and pains as 'the battle with the body' and they were to overshadow most of the next few days, in fact to be a continual problem until I learnt simply to accept them. By the time we reached our goal for the first day, about fifteen miles' walk, the feverish cold that threatened as we left Winchester had emerged; worse, it was doing its best to deprive me of hearing in one ear; my legs were aching and a muscular spasm in my back left me wanting no position other than the horizontal. And our meeting place, picked at random from Ropley's pubs, far from providing a warm, welcoming end to the day, was a cheerless place. Clearly the locals knew better than to patronize it, for we were the only people there as we drank the roughest of red wine and struggled through a greasy fry-up.

My spirits lifted slightly as we arrived at our first night's lodgings, a nearby monastery, spacious and still. Silence is kept after 8.30 and the guest-master, a charming Irish monk, showed us round, delivering his familiar patter in a stage whisper. He warned us of the lighting system, 'It goes on automatically - rather spooky, but you'll get used to it' then took us to our rooms, pointing out the whereabouts of soap, towels and hanging space and opening a drawer to reveal sheets for the next inhabitant. 'In the morning you will change the sheets - not the duvet cover - and you will drop them, disdainfully (suiting the expression to the word) on the floor.' He told us that the monks are the servants as well as the masters and anyone who has used a washing machine will sympathize with his wish not to feed it with folded sheets. Continuing his merciless self-parody he sought our patience if the local wildlife disturbed us during the night, adding 'and if you walk in the garden in the morning, do not disturb the badgers, they're shy little people.' With instructions to meet him outside the dining room at two minutes to eight the next morning he left us.

Was I a pilgrim, a tourist, a retreatant? I had little sense of identity, more a slight self-consciousness, as I settled into the austere but comfortable room and unpacked before joining my companions for our evening meditation.

'And the evening and the morning were the first day.' I could not keep the rather inappropriate phrase from my mind.

THE 'LIMINAL STATE'

Chapter Three

Ropley Dean to Lower Froyle

Guilt and Penance

On Tuesday morning, at two minutes to eight, we were waiting outside the refectory, as instructed by the guestmaster. 'Orange juice to the right, cereals on your left,' he said. 'And when you've finished you will put your cutlery in the kitchen. Eat as much as you like now, you've a long way to go.'

Observing monastic silence we helped ourselves to the cereal and the four pieces of toast in front of us, then went into the garden (careful not to disturb the badgers) to discuss the day ahead. My fellow walkers argued, quite convincingly, that we should skip the three miles from Ropley Dean to Four Marks as one of our number had very bad blisters and could not walk that day, and that in any case I had walked that stretch on a previous occasion. I was split in two. On the one hand the fact that I had covered the ground before did not seem relevant, nor did I like the thought of failing so early in my resolution to walk all the way. On the other, to go against the consensus of opinion or to force my friends to walk in discomfort or against their wishes was an option I was unwilling to take. Perhaps I should put pride on one side and learn a lesson in flexibility.

Perhaps I should have done, but I could not do it. I suggested the obvious compromise, that I walk alone, but that was not accepted, so it was decided that the two of us so far without blisters should pick up the track where we had left it the night before. With me feeling guilty at getting my own way, we got out of the car at Ropley Dean, shrugged on our rucksacks and made our way up the road to the village of Ropley itself.

In taking this route we were deviating from the straight road ahead, now the A31, but we were in accord with two of the Way's most scrupulous researchers. Mrs Adie, who wrote about the Pilgrims' Way in the nineteenth century, agrees with the tradition that says the pilgrims would have passed through Ropley, and Belloc, writing a few years later, supports her, citing the discovery of Celtic collars, necklaces and bracelets to indicate the road's even more ancient use. Though this way is slightly longer, we were glad to avoid the busy main road and to enjoy this quiet country lane, passing through fields, to the south an old burial mound and a small copse. When Belloc walked this stretch it was an abandoned grassy path some twenty yards across, rutted by the passage of farm carts:

> It was treeless, wide, and the most of it neglected; never metalled during all the one hundred and fifty years which have transformed English highways. It was the most desolate, as it was the most convincing, fragment of the Old Road we had set out to find.[1]

Though now metalled, this lane still has a haunting authenticity and it was not hard to imagine the tramp of long-dead feet. But before fantasy could take over we were engulfed by the bleak sprawling bungalows of Four Marks, of which the less said the kinder. It has, however, a pleasant pub, where we met our companions for coffee and I recalled my previous visit. On that occasion, barely recovered from an operation, I had walked the eighteen-odd miles from Winchester in one day. I arrived exhausted, asking for a drink and boasting of my achievement. 'You must be mad!' said the barman. I had to agree with him.

Leaving Four Marks we crossed the Watercress Line, lamenting the demise of all but a few steam trains in the country. As the Pilgrims' Way almost certainly followed the route now taken by the railway line, we took a parallel path, through Chawton Park Wood to Alton. This was our first woodland walk and we rejoiced in it. It was that magic moment in spring when the beech leaves are almost translucent, trying to decide whether they are green or gold; when the bluebells are still alert, upright and fully clothed in flower. Our delight was marred only by a solitary motorcyclist, polluting the air with aggressive accelerations as he sped round the nearby motor-racing circuit. Yet even this failed to break my mood. I was touched by the macho use of battered old cars, in contrast to the huge budgets and publicity machines of the car-racing world, and the noise served less as an irritant than to highlight the beauty that surrounded us. I recalled Chinese art, always containing a flaw to remind us that man is fallible.

In this wood thoughts of Neolithic man and medieval pilgrims gave way to more recent associations. Jane Austen lived in the village of Chawton from 1809 till her early death eight years later. Here she wrote *Mansfield Park*, *Persuasion* and *Emma*. Her house is now a museum honouring her memory and scenes in *Emma* are believed to have been based on the surrounding countryside. At Selborne, only four miles distant, the Wakes Museum houses exhibitions in memory of two Englishmen, the naturalist Gilbert White and Captain Lawrence Oates, a member of Captain Scott's ill-fated expedition to the South Pole. Both, in very different ways, reflect threads of thought that are woven into pilgrimage.

The story of Captain Oates is of self-sacrifice in its purest form. He was suffering from frostbite and gangrene, he could not keep up with his companions and he knew that he was delaying them and endangering their lives still further. On 17 March 1912, in the middle of the night when they were asleep and could not prevent him, he walked out of the tent leaving a note. It said simply, 'I am just going outside. I may be some time.' His body was never found and Scott, Wilson and Bowers only achieved another fifteen miles before dying themselves.

Our trivial worries that we might delay each other with sore feet, tiredness and strained muscles were put firmly in perspective.

Gilbert White, by contrast, lived a quiet, unadventurous life, never moving far from the village of Selborne with which he is always associated and where he was, for several periods, curate. But his meticulous observations of the natural world gave his life a rare richness, and I was curious to know what his diaries would reveal about this part of the country two hundred years ago. The entries for the first week of May 1793 (incidentally the year of his death) show that the weather was unkind. 'Dark, rain, rain', 'Great rain, wind, and thunder at night', 'Sad blowing, wintry weather.' The beech trees were set back by this unseasonable weather, for he writes that they were only just beginning to 'show leaves', yet in other ways the rhythm of nature seems to have been unaffected, for he reports sowing seed, cutting cucumbers grown on beds of hot dung, notes the vines beginning to shoot and recorded seeing swallows, swifts, redstarts, housemartins and

> a bird of the black bird kind, with white on the breast, that haunts my outlet, as if it had a nest there. Is this a ring ousel? If it is, it must be a great curiosity, because they have not been known to breed in these parts. [2]

As the ring ousel breeds in mountain and hilly areas, usually above a thousand feet, it must indeed have been a rare sighting. Then there is a short, enigmatical entry about Timothy. Timothy, it turns out, was a thirty-year-old tortoise inherited from his Aunt Rebecca. Though whoever named it was mistaken about its sex (it was in fact female) White knew his favourite pet's habits most intimately, noting its voracious summer appetite, the long periods for which it can go without food and that even when first awakened from hibernation it eats nothing. Hence the triumphant entry, signalling the approach of summer, 'Timothy eats.'

We stopped for lunch at Alton, then, as the Pilgrims' Way was still usurped by the A31, walked round the edge of a school playing field to the village of Holybourne. Here we stopped to locate the site of the Roman town of Vindomis, discovered in 1969 during the building of Alton's bypass. It was hard to decide which of those carefully cultivated fields covered it, but we decided the mostly likely place was a field that, like so much of the country at this time of year, was a glaring blaze of rape. We then walked (carefully) through a fruit and vegetable farm and (uncomfortably) across a ploughed field, to Upper Froyle. I felt quite indignant at being again forced off our route. Somehow when we were on, or at least very near, the original road, there was a sense of belonging, of purpose, of identification with those who had walked before. Picking our way round private land, even though we were entitled to do so, made me feel intrusive, a stranger in my own country.

This sense of exclusion brought to mind something I had read about and that was now becoming a reality - that was the 'liminal state' in which the pilgrim lives. The liminal phase was first identified by the anthropologist Arnold van Gennep in connection with all rites of passage, which he defines as 'rites which accompany every change of place, state, social position and age'.[3] He showed that every rite of passage is marked by three phases. First there is separation, a detachment from all normal social structures; then the transitional or liminal phase (from the latin 'limen', meaning 'threshold'); finally incorporation or aggregation, when the passage is consummated. So the adolescent leaves childhood behind and goes through puberty before reaching adulthood; so too, before coming together in marriage, bride and groom have to leave their single status and go through the transitional state of betrothal.

Clearly pilgrimage, essentially a change of place and potentially leading to a change of state, is, like pregnancy, puberty and all travel, a rite of passage. In leaving our homes and separating from family and friends, in detaching ourselves from our usual surroundings and normal ways of life, we had been through the first phase and this had been ritually acknowledged in the prayers and blessing of the *Itinerarium*. But I had not fully absorbed this and the loss of identity I had experienced the previous night must have been because I had neither completely acknowledged this separation, nor recognized my new 'liminal' state. I found that being able to name it, to see that from the moment I left home until I arrived at Canterbury, I was in a recognizable phase, helped towards a new sense of identity. But this is not easy, for it is, as another distinguished anthropologist, Victor Turner, pointed out, an elusive stage, neither here nor there, betwixt and between, on the threshold:

> The liminal state has frequently been likened to death; to being in the womb; to invisibility, darkness, bisexuality, and the wilderness. Liminars are stripped of status and authority, removed from a social structure maintained and sanctioned by power and force, and leveled to a homogeneous social state through discipline and ordeal.[4]

At first reading this passage seemed very theoretical. What had this to do with us? Surely walking across part of southeast England could not encompass such high-flown concepts? But now, in my new role as a pilgrim, I found that I could enter into at least some of these ideas; I was, after all, living them. I knew that the sheer physical effort involved in walking would take up much of my energy and that I would only consciously understand a little of the profound significance of what I was doing, but I had a feeling that there would be deep resonances whose significance might not be revealed for a long time.

The only way I could relate to the archetypal pilgrim of which the anthropologists write was by simply being myself and seeing what happened; by fulfilling my determination to live in the present and leave everything to do with my normal life behind. I was already finding that the ties of normal life were loosening and I did not want to use the telephone, write postcards, even think about ordinary life. Tax forms, electricity bills, correspondence, shopping, social engagements, my garden, friends, even close relationships, must not – and, to my surprise did not – occupy my mind; the separation had to be as complete as possible if the riches I was convinced lay in the apparent void of the liminal state were to reveal themselves.

Turner does not claim that pilgrimage has all the attributes of liminality, but already it was clear that status and authority had gone, and with them many of the roles that we usually carry. There was no longer any significance attached to whether I was male or female, single, widowed, married or divorced; I was no longer in the role of employer or employed, consumer or producer, respectable citizen or apprehensive lawbreaker; I had few social obligations other than to my companions. So too, though I did not quite understand how, I was beginning to experience 'invisibility, darkness . . . and the wilderness'. The pilgrim has no secular responsibilities, no image to maintain, little choice of what he wears or where he sleeps. In his heart, if not in fact, he ceases to be a part of bureaucratic structures and inhabits a world free of driving licences, social security numbers and pension arrangements. He is not in competition with anyone and has no ambition but to reach his goal, though he does not know how, or even if, he is going to do so. Lost to the world, he becomes a mere speck of humanity, stripped of worldly ties, trudging along his chosen path. The idea of bisexuality eluded me, but comparison with being in the womb, being on the way to some sort of new life, easily became part of this new pattern.

It was a liberating experience. My only duty was to walk, to reach my destination. To achieve this simply involved, as Turner says, the discipline of keeping going and facing any ordeal, any physical, or indeed mental, discomfort that might come my way. What freedom, what simplicity there was in this realization. I wondered if it might become addictive, if I might want never to live any other way.

So we three pilgrims, content to be living in this dreaming space, this no-man's-land divested of worldly trappings, came to the village of Upper Froyle, once more on the Pilgrims' Way. My perception of time was becoming more fluid, less firmly defined by the passing centuries, and the pagan origins of the village did not seem so very distant. Roads and tracks crossing this area give clues to its ancient history. To the north is the Harroway, sometimes known as the Tin Track or the Drove, once a highway that would have borne the feet of men and animals for at least four thousand years; to the west the Roman road once ran from Chichester to Silchester; and our route, the Pilgrims' Way, still passes through the village itself. Implements from the Stone Age and the Bronze Age have been found in the vicinity; Coldrey Farm, just to the south of the parish, is built on the remains of a Roman villa and Norman pottery has been found on the very path we were taking.

The name Froyle is believed to be derived from Froehyll or Frija's Hill, the hill between Upper and Lower Froyle now known as Saintbury Hill. Frija was one of the wives of Odin, the principal god of the Teutonic peoples, who held court at Valhalla with his handmaidens the Valkyries. In the second century his cult prevailed over all others and, in the fifth century, when the Angles and the Saxons invaded Great Britain, it was his name they invoked as they set out. There are many myths associated with Odin, one of the most appealing being the two crows, Hugin and Munin, ('thought' and 'memory') who made daily excursions at his command, returning in the early morning to sit on his shoulder and bring him news from around the world. Odin (or Woden) is still part of our daily lives, having given his name to the fourth day of the week, Wednesday, as his wife Frija did to Friday. Her name originally meant 'well-beloved' or 'spouse', so she was well fitted to be the Norse goddess of love, protecting marriages and making them fruitful.

Upper Froyle is also known as 'The Village of Saints'. This does not reflect on the holiness of the inhabitants, but refers to the statues of saints we saw in the doorways and recesses of the houses, reminding me of the fantasy village of Portmeirion, designed by Sir Clough Williams-Ellis. The statues were brought from Italy in the late nineteenth century by Sir Hubert Miller, the last active lord of the manor, who lived until the beginning of the First World War.

Today, Froyle is dominated by the Lord Mayor Treloar School for physically disabled children, a fact curiously omitted from the 'Short History' on sale in the church. A hospital and a college were founded in Alton in 1908 as the result of a national appeal made by Sir William Treloar, during his period of office as Lord Mayor of London. In 1948 the hospital was absorbed into the National Health Service and the college developed into the largest independent boarding school for severely physically handicapped children in the country. In fact it became so large that it is now divided into two, the Lower School at Froyle, the Upper School at Holybourne. Between them they educate and care for some 290 boys and girls afflicted by disabilities such as spina bifida, cerebral palsy, muscular dystrophy and by handicaps resulting from traffic and sporting accidents. We saw many of them, mostly in wheelchairs, reminding me painfully of the last days of my husband's life, when he could barely cross the room without help and for any longer distance, like these children, needed a wheelchair.

We had intended to reach Bentley on this, our second day's walking, but Froyle had tempted us to linger and by the time we decided to continue on our way it was five o'clock and we very tired. As we had only planned twelve miles for the following day and felt we could make up the distance then, we arranged with our driver, who was sketching the church, to meet us at the next village a mile or so short of Bentley.

I was already so much in a walking mode that the speed of travelling by car came as quite a shock. The wayside flowers flickered past the window in a haze of texture and colour rather than brushing us gently as we passed, fields flashed by and the few minutes the journey took made a mockery of distance. The rapidly passing scene included a glimpse of Isington Mill, just south of the main road. Once a Saxon settlement on the banks of the river Wey, then a brick water mill with two oast houses, it was derelict until after the war, when Field Marshal Lord Montgomery turned it into an attractive house, adding a shelter for his famous wartime caravan.

On my previous visit I had noticed a 'b & b' sign on the road near Isington and had booked us in for two nights. This was not done lightly, for the true pilgrim would go always forwards, sleeping where he found himself. But it was tempting occasionally to have time to settle in and have a chance to clean shoes, wash clothes and hair; restful to have a morning free from packing up the car. We were to do this on four separate occasions, though I have to admit to a slight feeling of guilt each time.

In fact this was a day when guilt kept peering at me, reminding me how far I was from being a true pilgrim. I had felt guilty at insisting on walking from Ropley Dean to Four Marks; guilty at seeing our frailty in comparison with the selfless courage of Captain Oates; guilty (though only slightly) at stopping short of our day's goal; and now guilty at staying two nights in the same place. I was beginning to feel rather bored with myself for being so consumed by guilt.

Yet guilt has its place in pilgrimage, for though pilgrimage was not undertaken as a penance until the sixth century, the medieval pilgrim would often have regarded it as a penitential exercise. Thirteenth-century theologians distinguished between voluntary pilgrimages, undertaken for personal reasons, and compulsory pilgrimages imposed by confessors, bishops or courts of law. It was thought to be a suitable punishment for sins as diverse as murder, sexual indiscretions, forgery, breaking sanctuary and 'public irreverence towards the services of the Church'; while many undertook a voluntary pilgrimage hoping to find forgiveness. An eleventh-century king of France, Robert the Pious, visited nine shrines in order to 'evade the awful sentence of the day of judgement'.[5]

I have to admit that I was not making this pilgrimage in a spirit of penitence. I cannot see that self-inflicted pain does any good to anyone, nor that there could be any relationship between the discomfort of the journey and the forgiveness of my sins. Someone had once said to me that 'If there is no penance there is no pilgrimage', but there is a difference between making a pilgrimage as a deliberate act of mortification and finding that it entails a certain amount of suffering. For me pilgrimage was a journey of discovery; I was motivated primarily by curiosity. My guilt should have lain in feeling guilty, for it is an unproductive emotion. Rather than dwell on one's shortcomings, I prefer the robust view expressed by Aldous Huxley:

> if you have behaved badly, repent, make what amends you can and address yourself to the task of behaving better next time. On no account brood over your wrongdoing. Rolling in the muck is not the best way of getting clean.[6]

Modern attitudes to sin may often be lax, but at least they are healthier. Recently, after making a particularly contrite confession, a wise priest told me that for my 'penance' I was to say the 'Glory be', very slowly and carefully. 'Glory be to the Father, and to the Son and to the Holy Spirit. As it was in the beginning, is now and ever shall be; world without end. Amen.' Saying those words did more to help me understand the true nature of my sins and shortcomings than any 'penitential exercise'.

On arrival at our lodgings I was shown into a room normally

occupied by a teenage girl, at present at boarding school. Here was a room sparkling with glorious adolescent vitality, throwing our previous night of monastic space and austerity into sharp relief. The walls were hardly visible beneath the photographs of serried ranks of schoolgirls, posters of lusty young men, pop stars and loving couples. The flat surfaces were so covered with the treasures and trinkets and toys accumulated during fifteen years of childhood that there was barely a square foot left for my possessions. In the chair sat a huge fat teddy bear. I thought of the lonely life of the celibate monk and was torn between admiration and pity.

We luxuriated in hot baths before a supper of excellent home-made soup and adequate spaghetti (for which we paid an inordinate price) and went gratefully to bed. The next day we would reach Farnham, where the Pilgrims' Way at last finds a place on the Ordnance Survey Maps. After a frustrating day when we had barely set foot on the Old Road, it was a satisfying thought and before sleep overtook me I switched my mind off my guilt and thought of roads, from grassy paths to modern motorways. The Way from Winchester to Canterbury is no longer clear and straight, there are many choices and every day we had to consider the best way to go to avoid motorways, built-up areas and private land. Before we continue walking, let us take time to consider how the route was first established and the arguments that we considered in deciding which way we should go if we were to follow, as closely as possible, the way of the pilgrims.

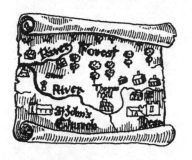

MEDIEVAL MAP

Chapter Four

The Wisdom of the Road

There is no doubt that the route we were following, from Winchester to Canterbury, is an old road, hallowed by time and the footsteps of men and animals. It may not seem so now, bruised by building, scarred by highways and motorways, yet, as we were already discovering, there are long stretches where nature is still allowed to breathe freely and where the imagination can be transported back through the centuries to share the experience of those in whose steps we tread today. Though much of it is very beautiful and surprisingly quiet, it is more than a pleasant country walk. The road does not reveal its secrets willingly, but I found that the more I learnt about its history the more I wanted to know, for unveiling the past enriches and intensifies experience.

To rediscover an ancient track is to be involved in conjecture, supposition, even guesswork. Many arguments, sometimes quite complex, have been made in favour of this turning or that, in determining whether the route would have gone through a particular village, scaled a particular hill. I sometimes found myself impatient of all this detail, wondering if it mattered *exactly* which way we took, whether it was not enough to know that we were travelling in more or less the right direction. But I was glad when I persisted, for those who had walked before us became more real as we knew we were passing the very places they had passed.

Of all who have written about the Pilgrims' Way pride of place must go to the prolific and versatile writer Hilaire Belloc.

He set out one cold winter's day over ninety years ago and mapped out, yard by yard, all that could be recovered of what is now known as 'The Pilgrims' Way'. His book, *The Old Road*, first published in 1904, is essential reading for anyone wanting to exercise their minds as well as their legs. Though he has been dismissed as 'an incurable old romantic', I do not share this view and feel he should be taken seriously, for not only did he, for the most part, take infinite pains to question and check every detail, but, more crucially, he did so with a real sensitivity to the habits and inclinations of travellers, entering into their minds and souls. He may not always be right – there can never be certainty about such things – but his arguments take account of spiritual as well as bodily needs; he is as aware of the symbolism of the road as of practical problems such as the best way to cross a waterway. As I recalled his theories and conclusions he became almost a fourth companion on the walk.

Belloc constantly reminds his readers that the road is, like fire, a protecting roof or a watchful tower, one of the 'primal things'. We may take it for granted, but for him it was

the humblest and the most subtle . . . the greatest and the most original of the spells which we inherit from the earliest pioneers of our race. It was the most imperative and the first of our necessities. [1]

Imagine untrodden countryside, a world without trackways, paths or roads, the huge forests and bare moorlands that would have lain before the first to arrive in this country. A delight to the naturalist perhaps, a challenge to the explorer, but daunting to someone doubtful of their destination and ignorant of the way. Consider too all that follows in its wake – buildings, commerce, information, communities – none would exist without the road. We respond to old roads as to old buildings; even their names – Watling Street, Ermine Street, the Fosse Way, the Maiden Way, Stane Street – echo in the imagination. I remember as a child being told, as we walked the Berkshire Downs, that we were on a Roman Road called Icknield Street; I remember too my pride thereafter in recognizing a long straight road as Roman. Still the thought of these roads conjures up scenes of a different world, centuries removed from the A31, the B3000, the M25.

A road does not just appear, it is the fruit of long years of trial and error. It is the supreme collective endeavour, a long experiment in which the individual can only be subsumed. And the road is wise. It takes us the easiest way, saves us from ravines, bogs and marshy land, prevents us arriving at a river that cannot be crossed, a mountain impossible to scale. While it may divide and offer bewildering choice, to leave it is to risk dead ends, false journeys.

So who would we be following? Who first trod this route, arching across the map and linking the two historic cities of Winchester and Canterbury, one a centre of temporal, the other of ecclesiastical, power? Belloc's concern is primarily to establish the route he calls the Old Road, for though it is now called the Pilgrims' Way and associated with the Christian pilgrimages of the Middle Ages, in fact the pilgrims were latecomers, only using it for some 350 years between the end of the twelfth century and the Dissolution of the Monasteries. There is plenty of archaeological evidence - pagan stone circles, heathen shrines, pit dwellings, Druid stones, burial mounds and megalithic monuments - that it had already been used for thousands of years. The first tracks could have been made by Mesolithic people and their animals some 10,000 years ago; it was certainly used by Neolithic man. Later it was travelled by drovers, traders and merchants bringing ingots of tin from Cornwall. Its use by the Romans is confirmed by villas, baths, pavements, coins, cinerary urns and pottery. It is probable that kings and courtiers, bishops and clerics, would also have needed to travel between Winchester to Canterbury and would have had little alternative but to use the same road.

It is even possible that Becket himself would have travelled this way.

Though we had decided to start from Winchester, for many that city would have been a stop on a journey starting from much further afield. In the Middle Ages, Christian pilgrims making their way to Canterbury came from all over England, from France, Spain and Italy. Normans, Bretons and others from the Continent who disembarked at Southampton would almost certainly have headed first for Winchester. Those coming from the West of England might already have stopped at Shaftesbury, to pray at the shrine of Saint Edward the Martyr at the abbey church; others coming from Dorset could have visited the parish church of Whitchurch Canonicorum, near Lyme Regis, where visitors still leave prayer requests and coins within the shrine of its patron saint, Saint Candida. Unlike us, they would already have been seasoned pilgrims.

When the pilgrims neared Winchester, they would have passed the Iron Age fort of St Catherine's Hill (though the maze I walked would not yet have been made) on their way to honour the shrine of St Swithun, where they would have prayed for miraculous healing; they could have found refreshment at the Hospital of St Cross, though it was designed for 'the poor of Christ' rather than specifically for pilgrims, and might have claimed the free 'Wayfarer's Dole' at the porter's hatch by St Cross Church. (This tradition is still observed, and even now travellers can request a slice of bread and a horn of beer, drunk from the very cups used by the medieval pilgrims. I tried one weekend, only to find that, with true twentieth-century bureaucracy, pilgrims are only expected to be hungry during working hours.) Perhaps too they would have bought provisions for the journey at Saint Giles' Fair, held on a hill east of the city from the time of William the Conqueror.

Before leaving Winchester they would have been shriven and blessed, then, cleansed from the weight of their sins, would have followed, as we did, the river banks of the Itchen and the Wey to Farnham. There they would have been joined by travellers taking the Harrow or Hoar Way from Stonehenge, one of the most important temples in Europe. From Farnham the Pilgrims' Way broadly follows the North Downs Way, joining the route that Chaucer's pilgrims took from London at Harbledown, just two miles north of Canterbury.

The Christian pilgrims had set their feet on a well-used track shaped by centuries of tramping feet, breathing the elusive allure of ancient use. Long before we set out my imagination was stirred by the way Belloc entered into the mind of those travellers:

> The pilgrim set out from Winchester. 'You must pass by that well,' he heard, 'it is sacred.' . . . 'You must, of ritual, climb that isolated hill which you see against the sky. The spirits haunted it and were banished by the faith, and they say that martyrs died there.' . . . 'It is at the peril of the pilgrimage that you neglect this stone, whose virtue saved our fathers in the great battle.' . . . 'The church you will next see upon your way is entered from the southern porch sunward by all truly devout men; such has been the custom here since custom began.'[2]

This is the stuff of poetry, and pilgrimage is closer to poetry than to cartography. The same force that drew our ancestors to rocks and springs and holy mountains draws their successors in its wake. I was disappointed that I could find no evidence that ley lines linked points of traditional sanctity between Winchester and Canterbury, but it was consoling that on the way are many holy places where man has worshipped his god. Belloc is convinced that the Way passed no less than thirteen churches. There must have been some significance in their position, for often Christian churches were built on sites previously used for pagan worship; it is as if the magnet of holiness attracted worshippers to a particular place, even if the god was worshipped under a different form.

Apart from the practical advantages of following a track already beaten into the earth, a track that will lead to points where rivers can be crossed, where water might be found, it seems natural that medieval man should instinctively follow his ancestors. Perhaps in doing so they performed a greater service than they knew, for Belloc argues that, with the decline of Winchester's importance and the decrease of traffic from west to east, coupled with the increased commercial importance of East Anglia, the Road would have disappeared. It was, he claims, the murder of Thomas Becket and the pilgrimage to his shrine that saved the Road. Thus the road once used by pagans developed new sanctities of its own and 'Our remote ancestory was baptized again.'[3]

The route we now know as the Pilgrims' Way was not so called until the eighteenth century and did not appear on Ordnance Survey maps until the 1860s. There is no documentary evidence confirming exactly which route the pilgrims would have used, in any case travellers would have taken slightly different paths according to variables such as weather and personal inclination. However, as an existing trail, the Old Road would have been the obvious choice and it is easy to believe that this is the route they took. While Belloc sought mainly to determine the route taken by the Old Road, he constantly refers to the passage of the pilgrims, even suggesting that 'A saint must have come to Canterbury. A primeval site will sooner or later bring to fruit a primeval sacredness.'[4]

How did Belloc plot the Road's course? First he read all that he could find, talked to geologists and antiquarians and studied maps, then, on 22 December 1903, he and a companion set out to explore the route themselves, carrying 'no pack or burden' and timing their departure so that they would arrive in Canterbury on 29 December, the very day on which Thomas Becket was murdered. Thay must have been

strong walkers, for this gave them only eight short winter days
~ fifty-six hours of daylight ~ which probably accounts for the
occasional lack of clarity and doubtful conclusions.

He considered geographical and geological conditions, he
made analogies with existing trails and suggested that place
names hinted 'though only faintly' at the history of a village
site. I had been excited to hear of place names still in use such
as Pilgrim's Lodge, Pilgrim's Ferry, Palmer's Wood, Paternoster
Lane and Pray Meadows, assuming they supported the idea
that the Road was used by Christians, but in fact these can
only be used as corroboration of medieval use, not proof. Place
names can claim a long lineage and indicate the history of a
site, but many a modern street or house has ridden on the back
of the associations of the area and adopted names associated
with pilgrimage ~ I noticed roads in modern housing estates
with names like Pilgrims' Lane. Similarly though the churches
on the route prove Christian presence, they can only indicate
the possibility of prehistoric sanctity.

Wells, particularly those regarded as holy, confirm the
presence of man and indicate use by travellers and Belloc was
also convinced that the presence of yew trees indicated the Old
Road. Here he seems to be on doubtful ground, for yew trees
grow all over that part of the country and their association
with churchyards is widespread; their absence from most
cultivated land can be attributed to the plough and the danger
to animals from their poisonous leaves. His argument that yew
trees prove the Road's ancient use seems further undermined
by the fact that claims for their longevity are greatly
exaggerated; a yew tree a thousand years old is a rare exception
and few of those along the route can claim great age. More
definite proof of the Road's use lies in the existence of
turnpikes, but the system was only introduced in the
eighteenth century so they cannot contribute to the
rediscovery of the prehistoric or medieval trail. Moreover, as
they charged tolls, many travellers would have avoided them
whenever possible.

Most of the arguments for plotting the course of the road travelled by prehistoric man has to be sought in the earth itself. The Road was not paved or embanked, its secret lies in the great masses of chalk hills between Winchester and Canterbury. While clay, sand, marshy land and rock leave no mark, chalk, firm yet not too hard, retains the trace of passage, over the years leaving the clear impressions that can be seen on chalk downs everywhere. It is also, as any walker will know, one of the kindest surfaces on which to travel. For early man the chalky uplands had a further advantage – they would have been safer than the great dark forest of Andredesweald which, until well into Anglo-Saxon times, stretched across the south-east of England and where they would have had to brave wolves and boars, thieves, bandits and wild men.

So it was in the chalk itself that Belloc found several characteristics common to all the known, or at least probable, stretches of the Road – a sort of circumstantial evidence. He collated these and from them deduced the most likely way the missing stretches would have taken. Filling in these gaps was eased by the fact that he was confident that sixty per cent of the Road is known and no continuous gap is longer than seven miles.

Some of Belloc's characteristics are arguable, for instance that the Road never turns a sharp corner unless forced to do so by geological necessity, such as a formidable rock, a bend in a river or a change of ownership or cultivation. This may sound like common sense, that where it is possible to walk freely the tendency is to walk straight ahead, but in fact the Road does sometimes turn corners for no apparent reason. Again he disagreed with the argument that fear of attack caused prehistoric man to follow the very tops of the hills; Belloc claims fear is not the only consideration and that the Road does not, by choice, climb high. This accords with the human instinct not to make unnecessary effort, only going to the top for some particular reason. For instance without map or compass, early man might have needed to climb some chosen height to survey the terrain ahead and, after the advent of the plough, he might sometimes have been forced higher to seek dry ground above cultivated land.

Then Belloc notes the habit the Road has of clinging to the southern slopes of hills and the northern bank of rivers, where it is warmer and drier; that when the Road goes right up to the site of a church it would pass on its southern side, though he gives no reason why it should be so. Finally he found - reasonably enough - that the Road seeks dry ground where water has to be crossed and that a hill would always be ascended by the shortest route; it is the motorcar that has led to modern roads zig-zagging round a hill to reach the top.

Belloc believed, and he may well have been right, that though many had written about the Road, no one, since the days of the great pilgrimages to Canterbury, had travelled it in its entirety. He revered antiquity, finding that the farther away things are, the greater their appeal; he wanted to recreate the past.

> For my part I desired to step exactly in the footprints of such ancestors. I believed that, as I followed their hesitations at the river-crossings, as I climbed where they had climbed to a shrine whence they also had seen a wide plain, as I suffered the fatigue they suffered, and laboriously chose, as they had chosen, the proper soils for going, something of their much keener life would wake again in the blood I drew from them, and that in a sort I should forget the vileness of my own time, and renew for some few days the better freedom of that vigorous morning when men were erect, articulate, and worshipping God, but not yet broken by complexity and the long accumulation of evil. [5]

I am not sure I am at one with Belloc in his conviction that early man was any purer than those who came later, though certainly life then was less complex; nor could I help wondering what he would have felt about the devastation mankind has wrought by the end of the twentieth century, feeling as he did about the period before the First World War. Nevertheless, I completely shared his wish to tread, as nearly as possible, where my ancestors had trodden. But now, with motorways rubbing shoulders with the route, with the route itself sometimes a highway and land where once the Old Road passed now taken into private use, the task is even harder.

My companions and I were agreed that we did not intend to be puristic to the point of masochism. Every traveller, every pilgrim, has some choice and who would want to walk along the A31? Where it was possible we wanted to follow where Belloc believed the Old Road lay, but where it was prohibited by change of use, or made dangerous and disagreeable by highways, we would follow the alternatives suggested by Alan Charles in his book *Exploring the Pilgrims' Way* and, without straying too far from the Old Road, take quiet paths and tracks.

So, one more traveller along this ancient and much used road, I knew that those who had been before me would never be far from my mind.

A CATHEDRAL OF BEECH TREES

Chapter Five

Lower Froyle to Puttenham
Uncertainty

On the third morning we set off at nine o'clock, rather later than we had intended, and Barbara drove us to Lower Froyle, where we had given up the night before. There was a cool wind and, though sunless and rather grey, the dry ground made for easy walking; but it was to be a morning when the route was as elusive as mercury, continually frustrating our attempts to follow it.

This set me wondering if the medieval pilgrims ever lost their way. I imagined cheerful bands of pilgrims, confident of the route and rarely tired, for they would rest whenever they felt the need. Reason tried to justify that unlikely fantasy. In those days much of the land would have been covered by fields (where the view ahead would usually have been clear) or forest (much of which would have been impenetrable, dangerous and uninviting) and there would have been few buildings; thus the path etched by men and animals would have stretched ahead, presenting all kinds of dangers, but leaving little doubt about which way to turn. Uncluttered by motorways and sprawling towns, pilgrims would have simply followed the road, confident that it would guide them round natural hazards like marshy land or steep hills and lead them to that point of a river where it could be crossed.

The dangers that menace the twentieth-century pilgrim are not brigands, robbers or wild beasts, but motorways, highroads and urban sprawl. Despite one of us carrying a guide book and another an Ordnance Survey map, (the Pathfinder,

2.5 inches to the mile) there were quite a few occasions when, in our efforts to circumvent towns and the roads that have been laid over some stretches of the original Pilgrims' Way, we found we had taken the wrong turning. The modern guidebook relies not only on map and compass, on permanent features such as buildings, railway lines, road surfaces and road numbers, but on more ephemeral landmarks – stiles, the crop that was growing in a field when the book was written, even a fallen tree that may, by the time you pass that way, have become furniture or firewood. Neither can our own absent-mindedness be ruled out; sometimes it was nothing more than lack of attention that led us astray.

As we made up the mile from Lower Froyle to Bentley that we had not completed the day before, three times we found ourselves with furrowed brows, studying map and guide book and wondering which way to go. Each time we had to ask for directions and each time the locals treated us with the greatest kindness. On the first occasion we were rescued by a passing farmer who noticed our dilemma. 'You're on the Pilgrims' Way, my love.' 'Yes, we're going to Canterbury.' 'Then you're going the wrong way, my love.' So we took his advice and crossed a path scorched into a field of corn, allowing us to pass without trampling on the crops. No sooner were we reassured by seeing the 'massive fallen oak' that our guidebook was confident would still lie where it had fallen, than we found ourselves in the middle of a nursery garden. The owner showed us through, generously refraining from pointing out the way we should have gone, and we rejoined the A31 at Bentley, one of the few places in which the Pilgrims' Way is identical with the main street. Again we were confused, and were put on our way by a man who told us we must see the church, it was very beautiful and he was churchwarden. 'Or rather,' he added, as honesty overtook pride, 'my wife is.'

These moments of uncertainty over the route once again brought home the parallels between pilgrimage and life. Apart from a few intrepid souls, most people long for certainty, yet live in uncertainty, so in planning the journey it had seemed important to leave some things open and flexible, to let chance and unpredictability have a place. If every moment was calculated there would be no room for the unexpected and I wanted very much to be able to let go of any need to be in control, to meddle with fate.

Confident at last that we were on the right road, we followed a path by the railway line and the banks of the River Wey, past a huge sand quarry and on to Farnham. The weather was neither too hot nor too cold, the walking easy, and my mind was free to roam. I found myself thinking of uncertainty, of events over which one has no control, the times of waiting and suspense that we all endure. Waiting for exam results, for the post, for a telephone call . . . I thought of a prisoner at the bar waiting for the jury's decision, remembered recently waiting for the result of a medical examination, feeling that it would be easier to cope with knowing one had to die than with this uncertainty. Most poignantly, most agonizingly, I thought of someone diagnosed HIV positive, wondering daily when the symptoms showing he has AIDS will develop.

During periods of uncertainty there can be moments of a sort of peace, of an ability to accept, but they are unpredictable and elusive. I remembered a time of terrible uncertainty, when my husband was having heart surgery, walking round the streets saying, half aloud, those wonderfully comforting words of Julian of Norwich. 'All shall be well, and all shall be well, and all manner of thing shall be well.' The words became a mantra, to which I clung despairingly. I don't think I really believed they would alter the immediate situation, for I knew that Dame Julian was talking at a level far higher than instant answers, but something of their meaning must have pierced the veil of my total immersion in panic, for repeating her words calmed me a little and helped me through the day.

So on what nowadays people call our 'faith-journeys' we

have to accept uncertainty as we have to accept doubt; in the long term nothing is more pernicious than trying to brush them aside. Those moments when doubts disappear have, in my experience, nothing to do with reason, but are a sort of grace. The author of *The Cloud of Unknowing* put it well when he wrote 'By love he can be caught and held, but by thinking never.'[1] As we walked there were moments, usually quite unexpected and freely given, when that indefinable gift of grace showed a fleeting face, when I felt suffused by love. Words are poor conveyors of these moments and I do not intend to search for them, but I was interested to find a theological definition of grace, and grateful to Thomas à Kempis for this passage:

> It is the teacher of truth, the instructor of doctrine, the light of the heart, the consoler of affliction. It banishes sorrow, drives away fear, fosters devotion, and moves to contrition. Without grace, I am nothing but a dry tree, a barren stock fit only for destruction.[2]

Though by then the sky had cleared and it was a sparkling day, with a heady combination of a fresh wind and brilliant sun, grace was far away as we approached Farnham. I was 'nothing but a dry tree', more concerned with aches and pains than with divine grace. We were preoccupied, for instance, by shoes. One of my companions had not worn in her shoes sufficiently before we set out and had been struggling gallantly with blisters and sore toes, so on the outskirts of Farnham we left her to catch a bus to the pub where we were meeting for lunch and the other two of us took a quiet riverside path to the centre of the town. By the time we reached the pub my own feet were aching so much that I shed my shoes under the table, something I believe one is not supposed to do. The threat, apparently, is not only of offending wafts reaching your neighbours' nostrils, but that your feet, released from confinement, may expand and resent further captivity.

Farnham is one of the finest towns in southern England and Castle Street, with its mainly Georgian façades, one of the broadest and most beautiful. The town dates back to the Old Road itself – Mesolithic pit-dwellings found nearby are believed to date from the sixth millenium BC – and though the age of the town is unknown, there are indications in the iron-age fort known as Caesar's Camp and in its name, deriving from the Saxon 'Fernham', a village among the ferns or brackens. Its long history is harmoniously reflected in a variety of architectural styles – the twelfth-century castle, the medieval inns where pilgrims and yeomen would have eaten and the Old Vicarage in Church Lane, once a hostel where they would have sheltered. There are imposing houses such as the eighteenth-century Willmer House, now the town museum and, a few yards away, Vernon House, whose Georgian façade conceals a sixteenth-century house and is now the public library.

Farnham is one of the few towns directly on the Old Road, which seldom passes through settlements. Travellers sought dry going underfoot, while settlements, built after the roads were first etched across the countryside, needed water and tended to arise close to springs, usually found to the south of the Way. The lie of the hills round Farnham has given it an important position at the convergence of roads, most relevantly for us being that here the Pilgrims' Way from Winchester joins the Harrow Way from Stonehenge. For thousands of years travellers reaching Farnham would have been able to determine the broad contours of the road ahead with confidence, for a ridge of chalk hills offers the traveller a route from which he would be unlikely to deviate. First the Hog's Back and then the rolling chalk ridge of the North Downs Way would lead us to Canterbury, and on, if we so chose, to Dover. But before we follow the road along the escarpment, we must do what many pilgrims before us would have done, drop down river for a mile to visit Saint Mary's Well and Waverley Abbey, another place where pilgrims could have found a free night's lodging.

Christian pilgrims would presumably have visited Saint Mary's Well for its water rather than for its associations, for the small cave where the stream joins the river was the home of Mother Ludlum, reputedly a witch. It was once a hospitable place. Travellers could relax on seats beside the cave and drink from little iron cups, fastened by chains beside the stream. These are long gone, but the great cauldron in which Mother Ludlum used to brew magic potions can still be seen in Frensham church. She was apparently a kindly lady, willing to lend her vessels for local weddings and festivities.

I wondered what the monks felt about their neighbour as we approached Waverley Abbey and walked around the carefully tended ruins. It was the first Cistercian house in England and was founded in 1128 by William Giffard, Bishop of Winchester, who brought a small group of monks over from France. Halfway between Winchester and London it was a strategic siting and it grew fast; in just fifty years there were seventy monks and a hundred and twenty lay brothers. It prospered for four hundred years, though it had fallen on hard times by the time it was destroyed by Henry VIII's commissioners in 1536, when it was valued at just £196.

The stone remains of the Cistercian Abbey, glowing in the sunlight against the river bank, are beautiful in the way ruins so often are, and this first romantic impression was enhanced when I discovered the names of the meadows. One, to the west of the Abbey, is still called the Saffron Beds, from the time that the monks grew the saffron crocus there; the other, where the monks took their recreation, is still known as the Parlour Field. The Cistercians, or White Monks, tried to observe a stricter interpretation of the Benedictine rule and lived in puritanical simplicity, earning the praise of the contemporary historian William of Malmesbury. 'These monks,' he wrote, 'have the surest road to Heaven.' Surely these stones must once have been the homes of monks leading gentle pious lives in idyllic conditions?

On both counts the reality, however, was rather different.

Perhaps the summer months at Waverley would have been pleasant enough, but the winters must have been piercingly cold and wet, for the Abbey was built so near the river that it would not only have been damp, but would frequently have been flooded. So too it is hard to reconcile the image of holiness perceived by William of Malmesbury with the reaction of the local people, who came to have an intense dislike for the monks, 'whose greed for land was overwhelming'.[3] Their rapid acquisition of land (the original sixty acres became over five hundred in less than the lifetime of a monk) was used for sheep, for which English Cistercians were to become famous. At its prime the abbey owned thousands of sheep, who brought such rich returns that they were known as The Golden Hoof. Not only was their wool exceptionally fine, but they provided meat, milk and manure. They even took the place of later agricultural machinery by aerating the meadows with their hooves.

There are many stories told about Waverley Abbey. There is, for instance, the mysterious lady known as Domina Johanna Ferre who is buried near the high altar. Who was she and how did she earn such a distinguished burial place? I was not able to discover. And the tale of the shoemaker, accused of murder and a fugitive from justice, who sought sanctuary in the abbey. At the time this was his right – once a criminal had taken refuge in a church he could not, unless his crime was sacrilege or high treason, be removed from it. But the unfortunate shoemaker was tracked down by three ruthless men and, to the cries and protests of the helpless community, dragged away. For thus failing the fugitive the abbey lost its treasured right of sanctuary until it was restored by Henry III, who had the villains publicly flogged in Farnham churchyard and the shoemaker reinstated at the abbey.

I had read about an entry in the *Annales Waverleiae* which is of particular interest to the Canterbury pilgrim. There is a specially marked notice of the Martyrdom of St Thomas, outlined in wax with the words Saint Thomas in red lettering.

As the entry is dated 1171 and as Becket was not canonized until 1173, this shows that the martyr was considered a saint in the eyes of the Waverley monks well before formal canonization was given by the church.

After lunch and a happy woodland mile under beech, oak and rowan trees, we crossed the river Wey and for a short while found ourselves on a tarmac road. Time spun a web around me as I became aware of links with three different centuries. In a field to our left some archers were taking aim at great green circles. Seen from afar they could have been knights from the Middle Ages or a band of Robin Hood's men. Ahead was Moor Park House, with its associations with Sir William Temple, whose home it was in the late seventeenth century and where his secretary, the Irish satirist Jonathan Swift, wrote *The Tale of a Tub*. Then I was jolted into the present to discover that it is now a finishing school. Here girls, many from Japan, learn English as a foreign language, flower arranging, musical appreciation and current affairs. I had not realized that there was still any demand for these once fashionable and expensive forms of education; in any case such worldly sophistication felt very alien. It was quite a shock.

It was good to leave Moor Park House behind and to be on the North Downs Way, now a national trail opened by the Archbishop of Canterbury in 1978. From here to Canterbury much of the Pilgrims' Way coincides with the North Downs Way and my spirits lifted at the prospect of spending several days on the flank of the hills, save where we would need to drop down to cross rivers.

Soon we were walking in a cathedral of beech trees and I found myself wondering at the nature of a holy place. Though pilgrimage is, by definition, a journey to a sacred place, I was overcome by such a feeling of awe that it was as if we had already reached our goal. What could be more holy than this stillness at the centre of growth and life? I found a yearning for solitude creeping up on me. It was no reflection on my companions – perhaps they felt just the same as I. Nor was it that I wanted the peace of that wood all to myself, it was more a need for solitude in which to absorb it. Though this need for solitude was familiar enough, somehow in the context of pilgrimage it made me feel rather ashamed. Thomas Merton wrote that the only justification for a life of deliberate solitude is 'the conviction that it will help you to love not only God but also other men'.[4] But why should one need solitude to find that love? Surely one should be able to find love in the company of those you seek to love or it is a mere abstraction?

All too soon we left the woods and were in the midst of expensive suburban houses and approaching a golf course. This was commuter land, the area known as 'stockbroker's belt', the butt of ridicule since the days of William Cobbett. This robust and passionate commentator on the English countryside had been both soldier and farmer and had been imprisoned for opposing flogging in the army; in 1832 he became a Member of Parliament. He was born in Farnham – the house in which he was born is now a pub named after him – and rode round much of the South of England in the 1820s, describing it in *Rural Rides* with a mixture of loving evocation and indignant, sometimes choleric, outbursts as he lamented the death of rural England. He dipped his pen in venom before writing of stockbroking, 'this vile paper-money and funding system . . . born in hell':

> There are hundreds of men who live by being the agents *to carry on gambling*. They reside here in the Wen; many of the gamblers live in the country; they write up to their gambling agent, whom they call their stock-broker; he gambles according to their order; and they receive the profit or stand to the loss. Is it possible to conceive a viler calling than that of an agent for the carrying on of gambling! And yet the vagabonds call themselves gentlemen; or, at least, look upon themselves as the superiors of those who sweep the kennels.[5]

As the daughter of a stockbroker, perhaps I should have felt ambivalent about this, but instinct won over loyalty and I had to agree with him. The only redeeming feature about this section was an old steam engine, parked on someone's front lawn. But even this spoke of nostalgia for what once had been England.

I must admit, though, to feeling envious of the weekday golfers, sauntering gently round the putting green, for by then the muscle spasm in my back was searing with pain and I wondered how I could reach the next village, still less Canterbury. We found a seat on the edge of the golf course and sat for a while, luxuriating in the bliss of stopping. It seemed that the greatest pleasure in life was to STOP, the only point of the agony of walking was to look forward to the next chance to rest. I was good at stopping, as we walked. I wished I could be as good at stopping in life; better at letting go, at refraining from precipitate action or speech, at shutting up and leaving room for God. Many years ago I had been deeply affected by a passage from Lao Tzu, an older contemporary of Confucius and founder of Taoism:

The world is ruled by letting things take their course. It cannot be ruled by interfering.[6]

I had no particular ambition to rule even a part of the world, but for months these lines were a constant refrain, trying to protect me from my manipulative self. For a while I even thought I had learnt the lesson, but at least now I know that it is a lesson that needs to be relearnt every day.

Somehow we reached Seale and tottered to the twelfth-century church, undoubtedly one of the places at which early travellers would have sought both spiritual and material refreshment. I went through the Norman porch and found two old men sitting in the choir stalls, one each side. They invited me to join them for evensong, but I declined, saying

I was just passing through. As soon as they started I wished I had accepted, for there was something infinitely moving about these two men reciting the age-old words together. After a few minutes I found I was drawn as if by a magnet to join them. I knelt (as much to relieve my back as to worship the God who allowed it to give me so much pain) and tried to follow what they were saying. I was still so deaf in my right ear that I could only hear the occasional phrase, but the atmosphere was calm and gentle as the words washed over me. Afterwards they told me that they say evensong together every night, just the two of them. This faithfulness shone like a little beacon of light.

My companions were waiting outside and we exchanged news of the day. Barbara and Jane had been to Guildford and Jane had bought some sandals, so at last her feet would have a chance to recover. But she was not yet fit to continue walking, so she continued by car with Barbara and we arranged to meet at Puttenham, a couple of miles down the road. It was by then 5.30, the rush hour was in full swing and the road narrow and, for much of the way, without a verge. We set off carefully, just outside Seale passing Shoelands, a beautiful seventeenth-century house whose name is thought to derive from 'shool', an old dialect word meaning to beg and suggesting that this was a place where weary pilgrims pleaded for alms. As the next house is called Monks Well I wondered if they were sent on there for a drink and a wash.

Miraculously I had found a second wind and was enjoying walking, but the yearning for solitude overtook me again, and I asked Eileen if she would mind if I lagged behind and walked on my own. She looked doubtful, but agreed. So at last I was alone, not in a cathedral of beech trees but on a busy road ~ at least it was the Pilgrims' Way ~ at rush hour. I was engulfed in the fullness of evening that, especially in early summer, precedes the dying of the day. The noise of the traffic was somewhere at the periphery of my consciousness; almost in a dream I kept clear of the cars.

My solitary ecstasy did not last long. By the time I arrived at Puttenham I was again aching and tired, my cold had become slightly feverish, the spasm in my back a hard knot of pain, I could hearing nothing with my right ear, unless a fierce hissing inside my head counts as hearing. Worse, I realized I had upset Eileen. She was waiting, distraught, outside the pub, convinced I had been run over and I think – she did not admit it – hurt at my wish to be alone. I felt guilty at putting my own needs first; irritated that so small a request as a wish to walk alone should put me in that position; simultaneously touched and suffocated by what seemed such an overprotective attitude.

My general dissatisfaction reached the point where I began to think of all the reasons why making a pilgrimage was unnecessary, even undesirable. I thought again of Lao Tzu. He did not need to travel, in fact he quite explicitly advised against it:

> Without going outside, you may know the whole world.
> Without looking through the window, you may see the
>   ways of heaven.
> The farther you go, the less you know.[7]

Why did I not follow this advice and stay at home? Why could I not be content with making the inner journey – why did I need to give it outer form? I began to sympathize with those people in the Middle Ages who felt the need to make a pilgrimage but, unable or unwilling to walk themselves, paid others to go for them, thus making 'pilgrimages by proxy'.

I thought of my garden, back in Oxford. I thought of the thalictrums and honeysuckle and my favourite *Allium Bulgaricum* and *Papaver rupifragum*, all just coming into flower when I left. Why had I left the peace of my home for this? My body was in pain, my mind in turmoil. Nobody had forced me to do this; to do it voluntarily seemed sheer madness. I must consider not only why I had embarked on this venture, but why the need to go on pilgrimage has been, for thousands of years, so deep in the heart of man.

THE LADDER OF SALVATION — CHALDON CHURCH

Chapter Six

The Golden Thread

Pilgrimage is not just a walk from one place to another, however seriously it is undertaken; it is an age-old impulse, imbued with spiritual meaning. I wanted to find out more about this universal significance, not least in order to understand my own motivation. And as I was walking a pilgrimage made famous in the Middle Ages, I wanted in particular to learn about the place that pilgrimage held in medieval spirituality.

Pilgrimage is as old as the earliest sacred shrines, in fact even older, for prehistoric man was inspired to make pilgrimages to natural phenomena believed to be holy – a spring, a tree, a great height. And it is universal. The Greeks travelled to the Temple of Zeus at Olympia and the Oracle of Apollo at Delphi. The great Hindu festival, the Kumbh Mela, attracts millions of pilgrims every year. An unofficial guesstimate claimed that in the three days of the 1989 festival 27 million pilgrims bathed near the Sangam, the sacred point where the Ganges and the Jamuna rivers meet.[1] In Buddhism the search for images and relics of Buddha is regarded as an important first step on the road to enlightenment. Japan's most famous pilgrimage route takes the pilgrim to 88 Buddhist temples on the island of Shikoku, the number 88 being thought to represent the 88 'evil passions' which are eradicated, one by one, as each temple is visited. For Muslims a visit to Mecca is a duty proclaimed by Mohammed himself; indeed the constant stream of pilgrims has led to the birthplace of the Prophet becoming the centre of the whole Muslim world. The Jews have suffered perpetual pilgrimage and Christ, at twelve years old, went 'as usual' on pilgrimage to Jerusalem. We twentieth-century Britons were not unusual in wanting to make a pilgrimage, we were simply the latest recruits in an old and honoured tradition.

The three wise men following the star to pay homage to the newly-born Christ-child must surely rank as pilgrimage – what goal could be more sacred than the incarnated God himself? – yet early Christianity was a religion with no temples, no ceremony, no sanctuaries; for its first two hundred years there were no pilgrimages. But it was not long before devotion to the memory of Jesus led to Christians seeking out places invested with memories of his earthly life and in the third century two bishops travelled from Cappadocia in Asia Minor to Palestine to visit the holy sites. The history of Christian pilgrimage had begun.

In the fourth century, after the Emperor Constantine had embraced Christianity, his mother St Helena, who was in the habit of taking cakes, bread and wine to the shrines of saints, travelled – she was over seventy years old by then – to Jerusalem, where she is reputed to have found the most sacred relic of all, the Cross on which Jesus was crucified. Soon monks and nuns followed her example, so enthusiastically that they came to consider that a journey to Jerusalem was their sacred duty. This exaggerated view provoked energetic protests, particularly from the outspoken theologian Gregory of Nyssa, who remarked that he had found the gospels silent on the subject of pilgrimage and continued:

> Pilgrimages are to places held to be sacred, whereas particular places are not of any special importance in Christianity; what is of central importance is relationship with God and with people.[2]

It seemed to me that Gregory of Nyssa, in similar vein to Lao Tzu before him, had touched on something very important;

certainly it was a question that had preoccupied me from the moment I thought of making a pilgrimage myself. Why should we make physical journeys in search of spiritual goals? The fact that I had never before made a pilgrimage owes much to the fact that it is the inner journey that excites me. If God is everywhere, why should it be necessary to travel wearisome miles to find him? He is there already, in the countryside, in other people, in one's own heart. Yet faced with this blanket condemnation of pilgrimage I was curiously uneasy. Even leaving aside the parallels between the outer and the inner journey, surely it is natural to be drawn towards a place where God is thought to be particularly present? While it is impossible to argue with Gregory's emphasis on relationship, it seems a bit perverse to claim that place has no importance in a religion which has at its centre a birth in a known time and place. If we honour the birthplace of writers, artists and political leaders, how much more should we honour the place where it is believed that the son of God was born. Given Gregory's tendency to polemical outbursts, perhaps one should assume it was not the act of pilgrimage itself to which he objected, but rather that he was warning against its misuse.

At all events no one paid much attention to his injunctions. Pilgrimage became increasingly popular as Christians flocked to any site associated with Christ or his apostles. They went not only to the Holy Land and to Rome, but to the birthplaces of saints, the tombs of martyrs, to sites with a special association with the Mother of God. By the Middle Ages, the heyday of the pilgrimage to the shrine of Thomas Becket, pilgrimage had become one of the most popular expressions of man's yearnings for the divine. The thread of pilgrimage is one of the brightest and strongest in the tapestry of life in the Middle Ages, inextricably entwined with the phenomenon of medieval piety.

Royalty and commoners, palmers and pardoners, lawyers and knights, rascals and righteous, thieves and cutpurses, friars and laymen, parsons and paupers, Tom, Dick and Mary

~ every social class could be found in the groups of travellers wending their dusty way to holy shrines. Diverse as they were, they were bound together by an intense piety, strange when viewed from our rational age but then as inevitable as sunrise. For them evil was tangible and the Devil might accost sinners in the form of a spider, a goat or a savage dog; he could cause women to gossip during Mass. Most crucially, he vied with God for the soul of man, adrift on the ocean of vice and sin. Hell and its everlasting fires were a reality; at its gates were demonic hordes, waiting to catch the souls of sinners; in its bowels the angry were dismembered alive, the gluttonous force-fed on toads. The medieval view of nature was pantheistic, so natural forces took part in this cosmic morality. A gust of wind could be the breath of Satan, a flash of lightning was the punishment of God, the eclipse of the moon presaged certain disaster.

I had read that a twelfth-century wall painting at Chaldon Church, two miles north of the Pilgrims' Way, gives a vivid insight into the mind of medieval man, so in order to avoid making a detour on the long haul to Canterbury, I made a separate trip to see it. It depicts the Ladder of Salvation and is divided into four parts, the ladder providing the vertical line and a dense cloud separating Heaven and Hell horizontally. Peruse this painting and enter the dark inner world of medieval man. In the bottom right-hand corner the serpent, twined in the branches of the tree of the Garden of Eden, watches Adam's fall and the start of human sin; from this vantage point he can see men and women, balanced precariously on a thin, spiky bridge held over the fires of Hell, nervously picking their way across. In the next quarter two devils stir a burning cauldron, filled with doomed souls; a demonic wolf is gnawing the feet of another group of sinners; a woman's hand is being bitten by a hound of Hell.

Look at the top right-hand section and see those who have avoided the Devil's clutches; they have struggled up the ladder and are met by two angels who lead them up the gentler slope that lies ahead. Now Satan lies bound and helpless, Christ has descended to his level and thrust a lance into his mouth. Finally, in the top left-hand quarter, the Archangel Michael is weighing souls and a recording angel lists his findings. Satan is at work again, making a final desperate effort to reclaim souls about to disappear from his reach for ever. Some he has captured, but the virtuous fly upwards, with angelic assistance. The duality of Heaven and Hell, good and evil, could hardly be clearer.

The fear of Hell pervaded daily life. Devils lurked round every corner. Man was helpless. God was in total control of the natural world and directed every moment of human life, from the failing of a crop to the death of a child. Everyday happenings were seen as signs of divine favour or divine displeasure; thus the fourteenth-century poet William Langland sees a gale as God's judgement on the people's pride:

> Beeches and mighty oaks were dashed to the ground,
> with their roots twisted high in the air, as a terrible sign
> of the destruction that deadly sin will bring upon you
> all, on the Day of Doom.[3]

In the face of these malign, uncontrollable forces all that man could do was to supplicate, to placate, to perform rituals to expurgate sin and save himself from the powers of Hell. One of the commonest forms of propitiation was to make a pilgrimage.

If the main object of medieval pilgrimage was to make atonement or seek healing by travelling to a holy shrine, there were other reasons which took people from their homes, often for long periods, many of them owing little to piety and bearing more resemblance to a summer holiday than to a lenten fast. Nor does the modern pilgrim have to search very hard to find a parallel with his own motivation. For instance there was the simple desire for a break. Medieval communities endured a suffocating lack of privacy, all but the richest living in such close proximity to each other that nothing could be kept secret from inquisitive and ever-present neighbours. Further, the parishioner was totally bound to his parish. He was not allowed to receive the sacraments in any church but his own, nor could he make his confession to anyone other than his own priest. How tempting it must have been to escape from this monotonous, oppressive life; no wonder a fifteenth-century writer suggested that the principal motives of pilgrims were 'curiusity to see new places and experience new things, impatience of the servant with his master, of children with their parents, or wives with their husbands'. To go on pilgrimage, which was not undertaken lightly and needed permission from the bishop, was a respectable excuse to leave home. Better still, there was the bonus of the dignity conferred by the apparently pious act and the pleasure of coming home, telling tales of foreign parts and displaying pilgrim badges. Then, as now, people liked to boast of their travels.

So pilgrimage became an excuse to leave home, to satisfy the spirit of adventure; indeed the guidebooks of the later Middle Ages show that pilgrimage had become as much a holiday as a pious exercise. The line between tourism and pilgrimage was becoming increasingly thin as warnings were issued that no one should go to the Holy Land simply to be able to revel in travellers' tales. The Dutch scholar Erasmus was in the forefront of those who denounced pilgrimages, referring to them quite explicitly as merely tourist excursions.

There were worse reasons ~ at least tourism can claim a certain innocence. Among medieval pilgrims were some whose main aim was to take advantage of free lodgings from monasteries and hostelries; to seek alms from wealthy fellow travellers; to beg, to rob ~ the cutpurse was a familiar figure in any pilgrimage ~ to have sexual adventures. An eighth-century letter from St Boniface to Cuthbert, Archbishop of Canterbury, deplored women and nuns going on pilgrimage to Rome, for he was convinced that very few of them returned intact, adding that there was scarcely a city in Lombardy or in Gaul where there were not several of these English pilgrims turned prostitute.

Sometimes pilgrims took to the road out of sheer guilt. The public way in which medieval life was lived meant that there was no such thing as privacy; everyone knew all about everyone else's affairs, whether adultery, bigamy, domestic quarrels or even women denying their husbands conjugal rights. Surrounded by knowing eyes, it was hard to live down guilt. A German Franciscan set off for the Holy Land admitting that he had not lived up to his rule 'and therefore I have resolved to go away to a place where the German language is unknown, and there I shall exorcise my sins from my wretched body'.

As many went for mixed, dubious, even nefarious reasons, so too there was a 'proper spirit' in which pilgrimage could be undertaken. The journey of the ideal pilgrim could be, and in the fourteenth century was, presented as an allegory of the life of Christ.

> The pilgrim's entry into a roadside hospice was likened to the incarnation in the womb of the Blessed Virgin. The dangers of the route found their counterpart in the passion of the Lord. The pilgrim may be betrayed and killed by his companions as Christ was betrayed by Judas and killed by the Jews. He may be betrayed and killed by his host, as Christ was welcomed into Jerusalem by those same Jews who later killed him. Robbers may waylay and despoil him just as the soldiers divided Christ's belongings amongst themselves. [4]

Naïve as this, on one level, may seem, it was a real attempt to relive the life of the Saviour, to take up the Cross and follow Christ. And there is no scarcity of evidence showing that pilgrimage was encouraged. A thirteenth-century document in Hereford Cathedral quantifies the right to pilgrimage: after a year's residence a canon was allowed a three-week pilgrimage within England and once in his life he might cross the sea. He was allowed a year for Jerusalem ~ presumably a sort of sabbatical. It was also encouraged for the formal remission of sins. Priests and bishops would send people on pilgrimage as a penance; indulgences (documents excusing the penitent the temporal punishment due for his sins) would be granted for a particular pilgrimage. This was officially recognized by a Papal Bull, issued in 1300, which decreed that anyone visiting the Basilica of the Apostles during that year would receive a plenary indulgence. At the other end of the scale, making a pilgrimage to St Martha-on-the-Hill in Surrey was granted forty days indulgence.

It is hard to fault some of the reasons that took people away from their homes and into often dangerous, at the least uncomfortable, situations. Trying to put myself into the mind of a medieval pilgrim I found sympathy, even admiration, for much of their motivation. Many pilgrims went in a spirit of real devotion to the object of their pilgrimage; some sought spiritual profit through the sacrifice and the danger involved in the journey; there were those who went in a spirit of voluntary penance, those who wished to give thanks, and those, possibly the largest group, who went in a spirit of entreaty, usually hoping for miraculous healing.

The great age of the pilgrimage was brought to an end by the Reformation, but its spirit was too deep in the human psyche to be entirely repressed. It was not long before some of the medieval shrines emerged from their enforced obscurity and in the sixteenth century new sites, like the 'Holy Mount' at Gorz in Austria and the Monastery of Montserrat in Spain (incidentally the inspiration of Wagner's *Parsifal*) began to attract pilgrims. Though in the eighteenth century many bishops and princes prohibited pilgrimage altogether, the nineteenth saw an extraordinary revival, most of the new sites being dedicated to the Mother of God. Of these the most famous was Lourdes. The dedication of the church, in 1876, took place in the presence of 30 bishops, 3000 priests and 100,000 pilgrims. The following year the numbers rose to 250,000, an increase reflected in pilgrimages made to other European sites.

So what of today, the age of cynicism, video games and easy transport? Has the golden thread of pilgrimage been broken? Far from it. While the line between tourism and pilgrimage is still thin (is a quick visit to a local shrine during a fortnight's sunny holiday a pilgrimage?) we still have that ancient need to take to the road, to seek out the sacred. Every year over 10,000 go to Santiago de Compostela as accredited pilgrims, walking, biking or riding, while another one and a half million arrive in coaches and cars. In 1992 five and a half million people travelled to Lourdes and Walsingham receives 20,000 in organized groups alone, not to mention those who come unannounced. At its peak Medjugorje received 80,000 pilgrims every day and pilgrims flock to Fatima, San Giovanni, Croagh Patrick, Lough Derg, Knock as well as to communities like those founded on Iona or at Taizé. Yet this enthusiasm is not reflected in regular churchgoing. It is almost as if pilgrimage becomes even more popular as churchgoing declines; as if pilgrimage meets today's spiritual needs in a way more formal churchgoing does not.

Yet pilgrimage is an archetype which finds expression in many different ways and trying to define the various forms it takes is rather like trying to capture an octopus in a string bag – restrain seven parts and the eighth will somehow escape. At one end of the scale little has changed, for instance in Argentina the people of Entre Ríos have a devotion to relics and statues which savours more of the thirteenth century than the twentieth. When a statue of the Infant Jesus goes from house to house all are eager that he should spend a night in their home; the people often promise the Virgin that, in return for a particular favour, they will make a pilgrimage, barefoot, for three years in succession. So committed do they feel to this promise that the missionaries find it hard to persuade them that a promise is not binding if it proves impossible. I have a Dominican friend working there who wrote to me:

> Pilgrimages are the order of the day. The people love them and whereas I used to despise them, I now accept them in the spirit of the people here or at least try to enter into their spirit. We missionaries are taking a very different view of these popular devotions. We're no longer trying to clear them up, rather we're trying to develop a theology of devotion.

But while the word pilgrimage still conjures up images of a religious activity, should some secular journeys be regarded as pilgrimages? A recent book argues that 'as pilgrimage is a product and manifestation of its social environment, it is liable to change with the changing preoccupations of that social environment.'[5] Some cultural heroes, even if their lives were less than exemplary, are today regarded as earlier generations regarded saints – the scene of tragedy can become sacred ground; it surely follows that those who travel to these modern shrines must be regarded as pilgrims.

A powerful example of secular pilgrimage is Graceland, the Tennessee home of the American pop star Elvis Presley. Every year hundreds of thousands of people visit his grave. They see stickers at the graveside proclaiming 'Elvis lives', take away grains of soil, a coin in a glass bottle, even talk of miracles at his shrine. While it is possible to see these young people as pilgrims and their activity as a form of pilgrimage, it is impossible to regard Presley as a saint. Yet his fans have virtually canonized him, certainly for them he is hero, martyr, victim and saint, just as surely as Thomas Becket was for those who acclaimed him eight hundred years ago.

After the Hillsborough tragedy, when 95 Liverpool soccer fans were crushed to death in an overcrowded section of the stadium, the press described the stadium as a 'shrine', the ground as 'sacred turf' and the visits made to it as a 'pilgrimage'. Idealistic Western intellectuals visiting Communist countries such as Russia, China and Cuba were once (before our perception of these ideologies changed) described as 'political pilgrims'; even Disneyland has been described by a Japanese writer as 'a sacred place'.

More understandably, and nearer to the religious use of the word, the visits arranged for the bereaved to the graves of friends and relations killed in war are referred to as pilgrimages. A visitor to Gallipoli after the First World War wrote thus:

> The endurance of the aged in the dust and blinding glare of the Near East sun was amazing. Side by side with younger women, widows, and daughters, and friends, some of these aged ones climbed through the rough scrub and tortuous ravines and barbed wire and over the old front line trenches and gun emplacements that they might know the manner of the country in which their boys and men fought and endured and fell.[6]

This passage captures the spirit of true pilgrimage as much as any walk to any sacred site. So too did a 93-year-old war widow reflect the significance of any spiritual journey when, after she had visited her husband's grave in France, the first time in the seventy years that had passed since his death, she could talk of nothing else until her own death six months later.

Whatever the dictionaries say, in the last resort definitions are sometimes subjective. One person's overpaid singer is another person's hero; a pile of stones to one is a sacred shrine to another; an uneventful walk to one can be a path of revelation to another. The symbolism is there; the everyday can be transformed by the experience. Though I would count visiting a pop star's grave more as a waste of time than as a pilgrimage, nevertheless for some it touches deep chords and stirs resonances of love that are not dissimilar from reactions expressed by people who visit places traditionally regarded as holy.

I searched my memory and talked to my companions about secular journeys we had made and felt could be honoured with the name of pilgrimage. One of them said that her instinct to go forward is so strong that she had never experienced an urge to revisit, to go back; in walking with us to Canterbury she was impelled more by curiosity about the experience than by homage to the past. Another remembers setting out from Dublin to Sligo to visit the grave of W. B. Yeats. She had gone alone, consciously making a pilgrimage in memory of a poet she much loves and admires.

My own thoughts turned to roots, revisiting one's own past. I remembered driving round Darlington, where my husband was born and spent much of his childhood. To him this was a sort of pilgrimage, despite his sadness at the changes ~ none for the better ~ that had taken place since he knew it. Then there was the occasion when we visited my own childhood home in Berkshire. Was I, in revisiting with John the place which had for fifteen years been the centre of my joys and sorrows, hopes and fears, making a pilgrimage? I think so. But only, and this was a distinction that was to appear again and again, in the goal, the arrival; in neither case was the journey significant, nor did it bear any resemblance to a pilgrimage.

The thread that connects pilgrimage throughout the ages is strong; pilgrims across the world are linked, even if divided by time and born into different religious cultures. The three of us, like earlier pilgrims, were seeking escape, change and adventure; so too did we hope to find meaning and healing, the sacred, 'the centre out there' as the anthropologist Victor Turner expressed it. Whatever our apparent differences, pilgrims are united in the search for spiritual nourishment. This is the thread that connects pilgrimage throughout the ages, the motivation that we share with earlier pilgrims. We may go to Lourdes seeking a cure, to the Holy Land to stand where Christ stood, to Medjugorje out of curiosity or in the hope of experiencing some manifestation of the Holy Spirit;

we may make a pilgrimage that appears to be purely secular. But we are also doing something more. Perhaps by doing it myself I might find out just what that 'something more' was.

ST CATHERINE'S CHAPEL

Chapter Seven

Puttenham to St Catherine's
Travelling light

I f pilgrimage is a golden thread that can lead us to our centre, our God, whatever terminology we wish to use, it is a thread which can become knotted and tangled, even broken. It is unlikely to be smooth and uneventful; and if pilgrimage is an image of life, neither should it be.

This needed remembering on our fourth morning, for I was in considerable discomfort and very depressed. Physically I was not feeling at all well. My cold was worse and I was feverish, my ears so blocked that I could hear almost nothing and any sounds struggling through my blocked Eustachian tubes seemed to come from another world; it was like being at the bottom of the sea. The spasm in my back was now hurting almost all the time, in degrees varying from mild to excruciating. To cap it all I had slept very badly and was still disturbed that my wish to walk alone the day before had so upset one of my companions. I wanted nothing more than to give up and go home there and then. I wanted it so badly that I hardly even felt ashamed at my weakness.

We discussed it over breakfast and I owe our continuation totally to my companions, who were made of stouter stuff than I and were determined to continue. So the flicker of light at the thought of home faded as we agreed to continue as we had planned. This meant Barbara driving Eileen back to Winchester so that she could pick up her car and drive it to Dorking. (She had devised a complicated plan for getting her car near Canterbury so that Barbara, whose route home took her in the opposite direction, would not have to drive us all the way back to Winchester at the end of the pilgrimage.)

This in turn gave us the option of leaving some of our luggage in Eileen's car. We had not anticipated doing this, but Barbara's car was very small and she felt that, on the occasions when it was carrying the four of us together with our luggage, it was hard on the car and uncomfortable for us. Though we did not mind the discomfort for the short distances we were covering in it, we accepted her concern for her car and sorted through our luggage, wondering what we could shed.

It was a fruitful exercise. We had all tried to bring as little as possible – how much further could we pare down our possessions? Could we try to follow the example of the medieval pilgrims in carrying nothing more than our immediate needs? Travelling light seemed an important symbol, and I had succeeded better than usual, though it has never been something I find easy. During the day's walk I only carried my notebook, guidebook, camera, some money and a small bottle of water, but I had appreciated knowing that in the evening I would be reunited with my suitcase. After much deliberation I parted with some clothes, with notes on the places we were to pass through, with books, shoe-cleaning things, even the candle and cross I had brought for our evening meditations were not essential. But surely I must have a spare pair of walking shoes, heavy though they were? And even though it was May, I could not risk having no waterproof clothing. Part of me would have loved to travel with only the clothes I stood up in and a toothbrush, but I knew I could not do it.

As I pondered over my possessions I was reminded of a dream I had once been told. The dreamer was floating down a river in a small boat, handing his possessions, one by one, to people on the bank beside him. Eventually he was left with only his watch. When he handed over that symbol of time, his time ran out and he died. Apart from the deep personal significance this must have had for the dreamer, I wondered if this dream justifies our need for possessions. It could be saying that while we are in this world, we need to have some of the things of this world. It is all a question of degree.

I felt purged and invigorated by this slimming exercise. On a walking pilgrimage above all, the less carried the easier the journey; it was to our own advantage. But a Hindu saying I had recently come across put another slant on travelling light:

Who indeed can run with a bundle on his head?
What the guru wants of you
is yourself,
and not what you have bought,
as you passed through the market.

I understood the truth of this and felt warmed by the thought of being wanted for myself alone. Yet steeped in the world and in materialism as I am, I needed the bundle on my head. I was well aware of how we clutter our minds with useless information, fill our homes with possessions, unable to distinguish need from greed; I know how the attraction of possessions pulls against the wish for a more austere life-style. Yet now, when shedding clutter had become not only spiritually desirable but a practical necessity, I still wanted things I did not need ~ the small pleasures of make-up and talcum powder, more than one change of clothes, one or two favourite pieces of jewellery, even my transistor radio. Walter Hilton, the fourteenth-century English mystic, would not have considered me a real pilgrim, for he wrote that

A real pilgrim going to Jerusalem . . . divests himself of all that he possesses, so that he can travel light. Similarly, if you wish to be a spiritual pilgrim, you must strip yourself of all your spiritual possessions; your good deeds as well as your bad deeds must be left behind. You must regard yourself as so spiritually poor that you have no confidence in your own actions; instead you must desire only the presence of Jesus, and his profound love. [1]

I liked the idea of stripping oneself of one's deeds, travelling spiritually light, leaving both guilt over the bad and self-righteousness over any good deeds behind. Letting go, something I have never been good at.

One of the thoughts which I still could not let go ‑ in fact which was to pursue me to Canterbury and beyond ‑ was the question of whether the divine is more present, more accessible, on pilgrimage than at home. If God was not to be found in some special way on a pilgrimage, why do we do it? Yet if he exists at all, he is everywhere and in everyone; there is no need to go on pilgrimage. The evidence in favour of pilgrimage being a way to experiencing God is quite simply us, the pilgrims. But many contrary voices are raised, for instance an unknown Irish author writing of 'a vain pilgrimage', said, 'Coming to Rome, much labour and little profit! The King whom you seek here, unless you bring Him with you, you will not find Him.' [2] In like vein an American pilgrim said, 'I've discovered I can meet the risen Lord just as well in Kansas City as I can in Jerusalem.' [3] Thomas à Kempis was scathing about the pilgrims of his time, observing that 'Few are made better by sickness, and those who make frequent pilgrimages seldom acquire holiness by so doing.' [4]

But walk we do. Pilgrimage persists. I was beginning to accept that giving outer form to the inner journey is an instinctive response to a deep human need; it is a sort of incarnation. The Jesuit Gerard Hughes, an experienced pilgrim, suggested that pilgrimage is a symbol that clarifies the nature of the inner journey:

The mystics make the inner journey in their own minds and hearts: pilgrims choose some physical destination, projecting their inner restlessness into an outer journey to some holy place, expressing in a physical gesture a deep interior longing of the soul to find its true destination. [5]

I could identify with this, the longing of the soul to find its true destination. And this line from Saint Catherine of Siena left me feeling quite intoxicated with revelation: 'All the way to heaven is heaven itself, because Christ said, I am the Way.'

Our luggage reduced, the decision to continue made, somehow the air was cleared and something bearing a faint association with energy filtered into my joints. I was further invigorated by knowing that today was to be a short day and that we only had about five miles ahead of us. (We had planned three of these 'short days', but in the event this was the only one that became a reality.) The drivers took off for Winchester, leaving Jane and me at Puttenham, taking stock of the village we had glimpsed only briefly the night before.

Puttenham is a pretty village, its cottages built either of 'clunch', a form of hardened chalk, or mellow brick made from the local clay. Belloc is confident that this would have been one of the villages on the Old Road, an argument supported by the antiquities from the Neolithic and Bronze Ages found at Puttenham Heath. There is also evidence of the passing of pilgrims in the age of the church, which dates from the early twelfth century, and in the winter fair, for many years held in the churchyard.

Many medieval fairs seemed to have been timed for the benefit of pilgrims, who would indeed have brought good business; pilgrims would replenish their supplies - food, clothes, utensils, weapons, candles and torches - and exchange gossip and information. Puttenham held its fair in winter in order to coincide with the passing of travellers aiming to reach Canterbury to celebrate the anniversary of Becket's murder in December. So too the fair at Shalford, a village we were to reach shortly, took place on the Feast of the Assumption, 15 August, to catch pilgrims returning from the summer festival, when the translation of Becket's body from the crypt to the Trinity Chapel was celebrated. For many years it was known as 'Becket's Fair'.

We tend to associate pilgrimage with penitence and guilt and piety, and indeed they were often serious affairs, but they were also about going to fairs and having fun, they were a break in the drab routine of life. The medieval pilgrims were a noisy crowd who would have been chatting, singing and joking as they walked along. They would sometimes have been accompanied by travelling vendors, showmen and mummers and when they rested by the wayside or stopped at an inn, they might have been entertained by gipsy girls performing sword dances, performing bears, or athletes turning endless somersaults. And everywhere droned the sound of the bagpipe, the hurdy-gurdy of the Middle Ages. But for some people it was all a bit much. A fifteenth-century writer living on the Pilgrims' Way complained to the Archbishop of Canterbury about the wanton songs and the bagpipes as the pilgrims passed:

> What with the noise of their singing, and with the sound of their piping, and with the jangling of their Canterbury bells, and with the barking of dogs after them, they make more noise than if the King came there away, with all his clarions and many other minstrels. [6]

The Church, however, took a more lenient view than the laity and saw no reason why pilgrims should not enjoy themselves. Arundel, Archbishop of Canterbury at the time, was firmly on the side of the pilgrims and replied with a gentle reprimand:

> Thou seest not far enough in this matter, for thou considerest not the great travel of pilgrims, therefore thou blamest the thing that is praisable. I say to thee that it is right well done that pilgrims have with them both singers and also pipers, that when one of them that goeth

barefoot, striketh his toe upon a stone and hurteth him sore, and maketh him to bleed: it is well done that he or his fellow begin then with a song, or else take out of his bosom a bagpipe for to drive away with such mirth the hurt of his fellow. For with such solace, the travel and weariness of pilgrims is lightly and merrily brought forth. [7]

We twentieth-century pilgrims were very boring, by comparison, but at least we were quiet.

Before we left Puttenham we visited the church, which would have had a particular attraction for thirsty and dusty pilgrims as there used to be a well close by the porch. Around 1750 it was filled in and for over two hundred years there was no trace that it had ever been there. Then, dramatically, on Palm Sunday in 1972, the contents suddenly subsided as a yew tree was swallowed into the ground and the well was rediscovered.

Belloc is convinced that the Pilgrims' Way passed to the south of Puttenham Church, through land now occupied by Puttenham Priory, an impressive Palladian mansion, and thence to Compton. He does not seem to have realized that a nineteenth-century owner of the house, more concerned with the traffic passing his windows than with pilgrimage, re-routed the road to the north; in any case even if it were possible to go to the south of the church it would now mean crossing the A3, so once again we were grateful to our guidebook, which took us off the road and into the North Downs Way. This led us along a quiet path to the north of Puttenham Heath and under two bridges crossing the A3, one a modern monstrosity, the other an old brick bridge designed by Sir Edwin Lutyens. On this bridge stand two huge wooden crosses, silently reminding motorists rushing down the modern road that they are crossing the Pilgrims' Way. It was a strangely moving sight.

Jane, now wearing sandals, was quite comfortable walking

and it was not long before we were at the Watts Gallery, just outside the village of Compton. George Watts, the Victorian painter, was married briefly to the actress Ellen Terry. When that marriage was dissolved he married Mary Fraser-Tytler, a wealthy young woman who not only devoted her life to him but, when he died in 1904, built a gallery as a shrine to his work. Here his pencil drawings, portraits, allegorical pictures and bronze figures can still be seen. She also designed a Memorial Chapel in the 'Arts and Crafts' style, planned as a Greek cross and rich in symbolic decoration – the labyrinth motif appears no less than five times. One, similar to the medieval Christian pattern, is on the altar, and outside the church are four angels holding circular shields, each incised with a unicursal labyrinth deriving from the pavement labyrinth at San Vitale, Ravenna.

I was struck once again by the ubiquity of the maze and by its persistence; it is found all over the world and can boast at least four thousand years of history. Mazes have been painstakingly engraved on rock faces, coins, doorposts and wine jugs; they have been carved in turf, laid in gravel pathways, outlined by hedges, pebbles or boulders. Mazes are still being built, there are Maze Societies and Journals and they are the subject of many books. But its particular interest for me was that in representing the journey through life towards its ultimate destination it is one of the oldest symbols of the inner journey and the fact that for Christians the maze is a symbol of pilgrimage.

On this walk alone there are associations with at least six mazes. There is the turf maze on the holy hill of St Catherine's, which I had walked before setting out; a pavement labyrinth is laid in brick beneath the altar of the church at Itchen Stoke, through which the Pilgrims' Way once passed; we were to pass quite near to a modern maze at Leeds Castle in Kent. Julian's Bower, the most celebrated turf maze in England, though far from our route, is connected with our journey in that it was thought to have been cut as a penance by one of the knights involved in the murder of Thomas Becket, and the mizmaze at Braemore Priory in Hampshire was constructed by monks who were supposed to crawl the maze on their knees as a substitute for a pilgrimage to Jerusalem. And now here were these strange angels, holding their shields in front of their bodies and reminding one irresistibly of the resemblance of the maze to human and animal entrails. In fact it has been suggested that the labyrinthine pattern originated in the disembowelling of animals and human beings for purposes of divination. [8]

After my experience of wholeness when walking St Catherine's maze it came as no surprise to learn that some mysterious claims are made for the maze, for instance that in treading the maze the walker may reach higher states of consciousness. It can also have ceremonial and magical use; it has been thought to follow the daily path of the sun; it has been cut as a model of the universe.

It is natural that so powerful a symbol of spiritual experience should extend to many other areas of life. It has been used to assist in childbirth, to protect fishermen and to adorn a garden. It finds a place in recreation, whether simply for exercise or in the traditional (and sometimes secret) game when the young men of the village try to reach the maiden at the centre, the successful youth claiming the girl as now belonging to him. Thus the maze symbolizes capture and defence, confusing the intruder and protecting the centre; the maiden is trapped while the young men are in turn frustrated in their efforts to reach her. And of course the maiden stands for the still centre, the goal of our pilgrimage, the end of our exploring.

There would have been no maze-bearing angels when the medieval pilgrims passed this way, but they would undoubtedly have visited Compton Church, dedicated to St Nicholas, only a short way further. The modern pilgrim should follow their example, for it is one of the most interesting churches in England, the tiny crosses on the

Norman window bearing witness to the presence of the pilgrims in whose footsteps we were following. It is very old, the tower and parts of the nave walls dating from before the Norman Conquest, and has some unusual features. One is a tall wide slit in the chancel wall near the pulpit, with a stone seat where the aged and infirm, unable to kneel on the bare stone floor, could sit, while still having a good view of the celebration of Mass at the altar. Hence the expression 'the weakest going to the wall'. Another sign of the past life of the church is a small square window, once leading to the cell of an anchorite, who lived walled up in this tiny space, watching the altar day and night and surviving on the charity of the priest and congregation for food and drink. Excavations in 1906 revealed six skeletons, buried one on top of the other beneath their cell, suggesting a tradition of hermetic use, rather than the presence of just one eccentric anchorite. I hope they were there by choice.

Even more unusual, in fact unique in England and possibly in Europe, is the upper sanctuary and its wooden balustrade, probably the oldest piece of ecclesiastical woodwork in the country. The purpose of this second sanctuary is unknown, though it could have housed a precious relic and the doorway, now blocked up but once giving access from outside the church, suggests that it could have been used as a pilgrim chapel.

After this short diversion the route goes, for two miles or so, through the woods of the Loseley Park Estate, home of the famous dairy products which bear its name. The magnificent Elizabethan mansion faces in the opposite direction to our path and we only glimpsed it occasionally through the trees, but we did not feel deprived, for this stretch was quiet and beautiful. The sandy path, straight and clear, spared us endless consultations with the map; the ground rose slightly on each side, wrapping us in a circle of brown earth and fallen leaves below, arching green branches above. Walking in companion able silence, easily and for once free of backache, the leaves and branches floating gently across the periphery of my vision, I was half-hypnotized by the steady tramp, tramp, tramp. It had the quality of a dream and I thought of the invisible pathways across Australia, the Songlines, and of the Aborigines ritually singing the Ancestors' songs, charging the world with new life. Like the barefoot Mahmoud in Bruce Chatwin's *The Songlines*:

> I never saw anything like the lightness of his step and, as he walked, he sang: a song, usually, about a girl from Wadi Hammamat who was lovely as a green parakeet. The camels were his only property. He had no flocks and wanted none. He was immune to everything we would call 'progress'.[9]

It was too good to last. 'Progress' interrupted us as all too soon we emerged on a tarmac road, a hill to the left covered with houses. 'Where are we?' I asked a pleasant-looking man, walking his dogs. 'Here,' he replied, enigmatically. 'Yes, I know. But where's here?' I persisted. It was Guildford. That lovely track, that hypnotic walk, was in the stockbroker belt, within yards of a big suburban city. I did not know Surrey possessed such tranquil corners; I would never be rude about the county again.

We had only to cross the road and go up a short sandy hill and we had reached our destination for the day – the recently cleaned ruins of St Catherine's Chapel, standing in dramatic silhouette on the top of a small hill. Opinions are divided as to whether this would have been on the medieval route. The notice at the foot of the hill assured us that it was not, but there are contrary arguments. As in Compton Church, it is possible that there was once a venerated relic on its upper floor, a belief based partly on the remains of no less than five doorways into a small chapel. Were they hewn out of the walls to give access to queues of pilgrims, seeking cures, offering their devotion? Then there is the existence, since 1308, of yet another fair, lasting for five days and surely an attraction to pilgrims. A spring at the foot of the hill, believed to have miraculous healing powers, would also have been irresistible to the medieval pilgrim. But the most powerful argument in favour of Saint Catherine's being on the route is the chapel's geographical position. It is built on the highest vantage point in the area and has a commanding view of the winding course of the river Wey immediately below, the rough marshy ground the other side and St Martha's Hill a couple of miles away. It would have been a natural place from which to survey the view up and down the valley and to consider where the river could be crossed.

We had lunch at an unassuming but excellent pub on the main road and then spent a contented hour sitting on the sandy beach by the side of the river watching boats, swans and ducks drifting past. Just to our left there is a fairly recent footbridge, which we would cross the next day and where Hilaire Belloc admitted to a piece of very curious behaviour. When he passed this way there was no bridge and he arrived after dark and too late for the ferry. This did not deter him. He and his companion clambered down the hill and stole a boat that lay moored on the bank. Using a walking stick for an oar they reached the other side, to the accompaniment of outraged protests from the woman who owned the boat. They pleaded 'grave necessity', put some money in the boat and departed with all speed and, I imagine, little dignity.

We celebrated our 'short day' by going into Guildford. I was still feeling physically unwell, queasy, faint and very deaf, but it had been a good day's walk. Despite dipping into the twentieth century to visit the hairdresser and taking a taxi to the Maryvale Pastoral Centre where we were to spend the night, I was beginning to feel more like a pilgrim, less like a tourist, though still not entirely sure how I made the distinction. The authorities at Santiago de Compostela are, however, quite clear; they define 'real' pilgrims as those who have walked, cycled or ridden on horseback for at least 150 kilometres. They are given free meals and a signed document, known as a 'Compostela'. Those who travel by bus, coach or car receive neither.

No serious pilgrim wants to be written off as a tourist, but it is possible not only to sympathize with Erasmus in denouncing some pilgrimages as secular excursions, but to argue that tourism can be a form of secular pilgrimage. David Lodge does just this. Roger Sheldrake, the anthropologist, in Lodge's novel *Paradise News*, was working on a thesis suggesting that sightseeing is a substitute for religious ritual.

> Accumulation of grace by visiting the shrines of high culture, souvenirs as relics. Guidebooks as devotional aids. You get the picture . . . tourism is the new world religion. Catholics, Protestants, Hindus, Muslims, Buddhists, atheists – the one thing they have in common is they all believe in the importance of seeing the Parthenon. Or the Sistine Chapel, or the Eiffel Tower.[10]

But sometimes the tourist becomes a pilgrim simply because of the depth of his experience. A Glastonbury resident expressed it like this:

> Sometimes they can come as tourists, who want just to be observers, you know, just to take pictures and move on, and they end up getting an experience they hadn't bargained for . . . which I think is the difference between tourism and pilgrimage, because pilgrims are going for an *experience*, and tourists are just going to have a look and a more superficial experience.[11]

So the tourist can become a pilgrim. I remember going to the Parthenon as a tourist, but moved to the depths of my being by the experience, I left as a pilgrim. Walking to Canterbury I had set out as a pilgrim and was slipping more and more comfortably into the role. It had, I think, something to do with feeling completely remote from my ordinary life, far more than on an ordinary holiday, of being immersed in what was happening moment by moment and of being aware of a sense of purpose, of going somewhere, having a destination, though it seemed a long way away.

VIEW FROM ST MARTHA'S

Chapter Eight

St Catherine's to
The Stepping Stones

A Golden Day

The fifth day of the pilgrimage was to take us 570 feet above sea level to St Martha's Chapel, crowning the hill we had seen from St Catherine's the day before. The two churches, the two hills, are only a short distance apart. Standing together yet separate, answering and responding to each other geographically, they are also linked in legend. One tells of how the first buildings were begun in the valley below and how each day's work was carried up the hill by fairies. Another, on more heroic scale, recalls how the stone for the twin churches was hewn by two giantesses, who had only one huge hammer between them. They would share it, hurling the great tool across the valley when the other had need of it. I wondered if they ever missed and the massive hammer fell to the ground beneath.

Starting from the foot of St Catherine's Hill where we had rested the previous day, we crossed the bridge over the piece of river made famous by Belloc's theft and passed to the north of Shalford, where John Bunyan is thought to have once lived in a cottage called Horn Hatch. Slender though the evidence might be, this wisp of a possibility has led to suggestions that the Slough of Despond in Bunyan's great classic *The Pilgrim's Progress* was based on the marshy valleys around Shalford; that its famous August fair was the prototype for Vanity Fair; even that it was the Pilgrims' Way from Winchester to Canterbury that gave him the idea for his allegory. It is a nice idea, even if unsustainable.

Shafts of sunlight were streaming through the branches of the trees as we skirted Chantries Wood before reaching the car park at the foot of St Martha's Hill. From there it was less than half a mile up the sandy path through the woods and we were standing on a site that has been a place of worship for thousands of years. It would have taken a lot to convince me that we were not standing where pilgrims had stood, so wrapped were we in the webs of history.

The early history of St Martha's Hill is lost to us. A few prehistoric flints are the only clues to a belief that heathen rites were practised there; the great rings of earth to the south of the church, possibly Druids' Circles, more probably an Iron Age Fort, have led some to put forward (and others to demolish) an argument that there had once been an ancient labyrinth etched in the side of the hill. Later, and more confident, is the tradition of festivities that took place in an area known as Ben Piece or Bent Piece, an area of greensward at the foot of the hill. An eyewitness account in *The Times* newspaper of April 18, 1870, tells of the custom, whose origins are 'lost in the obscurity of time'. Every Good Friday would see a pilgrimage to St Martha's:

> Thither, from all over the countryside, youths and maidens, old folks and children betake themselves, and gathered together on one of the most beautiful spots in Surrey, in full sight of the old Norman church which crowns the green summit of the hill, beguile the time with music and dancing.[1]

The paper does not mention that during the fifteenth and early sixteenth centuries those who made the pilgrimage to St Martha's Church earned themselves a 40 days 'indulgence', the remission of the punishment still due, (even after the penitent's sins had been sacramentally absolved), given by the Church and won through the merits of Christ and his saints. A fairly recent convert to Roman Catholicism myself, I still have a Protestant revulsion at such ideas ~ as indeed have many 'cradle' Catholics. I was more moved by the pilgrims' crosses, incised into the old nave doorway, sometimes with a second beside it, proudly showing that the pilgrim had returned by the same route. They acted as a reminder that in visiting this site we too were making a small pilgrimage inside the longer walk; one whose rewards far outstripped the small effort of climbing the hill.

There has been a church here for over a thousand years, and though nothing now remains of the original Saxon building, some twelfth-century masonry was left when it was rebuilt in 1848, leaving a heavy Norman-style church, only just worthy of its site. We wandered round, soaking in the atmosphere, trying to work out how many counties were spread before us ~ the pamphlet on sale at the church claims that the view takes in parts of eight. Certainly the view extends over Surrey into Sussex (was that the sea at the edge of the horizon?), Middlesex to the north, back into Hampshire to the west and towards Kent to the east. To find three more seemed to be more an exercise in imagination than geography.

Saint Martha's is still a living church, seating 110 people and holding services every Sunday, but the congregation must be reasonably fit, as the last part must be done on foot, cars only being allowed up to the church for weddings and funerals. And what a place to be buried! The actress Yvonne Arnaud and General Bernard Freyberg VC, who fought at Gallipoli, are among those who rest there.

The name borne by the hill and the church has no association with Saint Martha, though Saint Martha of Bethany, sister of Mary and Lazarus, is patron saint of the church and her day is kept on 29 July. It is in fact a corruption of Martyr's Hill, as it is thought that in about the year AD 600 Christians were martyred here. This led to thoughts about martyrs, something often in my mind ~ after all our destination was a martyr's shrine.

The word 'martyr' was originally used of the Apostles who

witnessed Christ's life and resurrection, but with the spread of persecution it came to be reserved for those who had undergone hardships for their faith, finally for those who had died for it. 'The blood of the martyrs is the seed of the Church,' said Tertullian in the third century. Who could deny the courage of the early Christians thrown to the lions rather than deny their faith? Who could argue that, in standing up to be counted, they set an example and brought others to share their faith?

Such courage is beyond my understanding, though there was one occasion when I could imagine having to choose extreme suffering rather than deny one's faith. It was when I was given a personal mantra for meditation and told never to say it aloud, to myself or anyone else. I could not imagine any circumstances in which I would have said that word. It was a vehicle for my own inner journey, my most private and special possession; having promised not to reveal it, I simply could not have done so. But I was not put to the test. If I had been I would almost certainly have clambered onto the chicken run to safety.

Yet I have always felt rather divided about martyrdom, suspecting that there are occasions when martyrdom is deliberately sought; wondering if there is a desire to be remembered as a hero. Knowing also that the idealism that can produce martyrs can also be devotion to a cause rather to the truth; the suicide bomber may be a martyr for his cause, to the other side he is a murderer. Struggling with these ambivalences, I was pleased to discover recently that I was in the excellent company of the Indian Jesuit Anthony de Mello:

Martyrs bother me. I think they're often brainwashed. Muslim martyrs, Hindu martyrs, Buddhist martyrs, Christian martyrs, they are brainwashed! They've got an idea in their heads that they must die, that death is a great thing. They feel nothing, they go right in. But not all of them . . .[2]

And there's the point – 'Not all of them.' There are some martyrs whose courage commands mystified admiration. For instance the Polish Catholic priest Maximilian Kolbe, a prisoner at Auschwitz. One hot day in the summer of 1941 ten men were being arbitrarily selected to be buried alive in airless concrete bunkers. As the finger was pointed at the ninth man, he cried out, 'My wife, my children, I shall never see them again!' At this Kolbe calmly stepped out of line, stood to attention before the deputy camp commandant and asked if he could take his place. I cannot think of Kolbe without my pulses quickening in awe. That he should have been canonized just 41 years later gives meaning to the whole concept of martyrdom. I found myself back full circle, scepticism giving way to admiration; wondering at the courage shown on this Surrey hill fourteen hundred years ago.

Saint Martha's was the parish church of Chilworth, once the site of two industries – the powder mills, the source of an explosion which caused the collapse of the old tower of the church in 1745, and a paper mill, whose product was used for treasury- and bank-notes. Both industries have long disappeared; both disfigured the landscape in Cobbett's day and were castigated by him:

> This valley, which seems to have been created by a bountiful providence, as one of the choicest retreats of man, has been, by ungrateful man, so perverted as to make it instrumental in carrying into execution two of the most damnable of purposes; in carrying out two of the most damnable inventions that ever sprang from the minds of man under the influence of the devil! namely, the making of *gunpowder* and of *bank notes*! . . . To think that these springs which God has commanded to flow from the side of these happy hills, for the comfort and the delight of man; to think that these springs should be perverted into means of spreading misery over a whole nation; and that too, under the base and hypocritical

pretence of promoting its *credit* and maintaining its *honour* and its *faith*. [3]

I often wondered what people like Cobbett and Belloc, who so deplored what man had done to the English countryside when they travelled it in the nineteenth and early twentieth centuries, would think of what we have managed to achieve in despoilation since then. Here, however, was a rare place where the last case was, at least marginally, better than the first. From our high point on St Martha's Hill we could see no signs of industry besmirching the countryside surrounding us.

We sat in the sun outside the church chatting until we suddenly realized we had lingered too long at this seductive site and needed to keep going if we were to reach Shere by lunch time. So we continued down the other side of the hill, soon leaving the North Downs Way and walking through an oak plantation and across the top of Weston Wood. The path was straight, narrow and once again sandy; smooth underfoot, but with the roughness of a real country way. It seemed so authentic a pilgrim route that I ceased to bother if it really was the Pilgrims' Way or not, though at this point it is confidently believed to be so.

At the far edge of the wood the Pilgrims' Way crosses Albury Street, where a left turn leads to the Silent Pools. Intrigued by the name, I was disappointed to find that far from being a place for quiet meditation it is sombre and gloomy. There were not many people there at the time, but it had that unmistakable feel of a much-visited place, calling to mind the remark ~ was it Logan Pearsall Smith's? ~ that mountains are spoiled by being 'too much stared at'. It is curious that the eye can be as invasive as the foot. Whatever the reason, I found it quite hard to picture the scene set in the Silent Pools by Martin Tupper, a nineteenth-century local novelist buried at Albury. He writes of a beautiful maiden who was swimming there naked when she was surprised by King John, who called to her to come out. Too embarrassed to obey him, she waded deeper and deeper into the pool until, letting out a great cry, she drowned. They say that on a moonlit night you can still hear her cry echoing across the water. I doubt whether she would have been tempted into the murky water today.

Returning to the road we saw an ornate Victorian Gothic building, an 'Irvingite' church built in 1840 for a sect called the Catholic Apostolic Church, but no longer used for services. Edward Irving, a close associate of the sect, was a Scottish minister who was excommunicated in 1830 for declaring Christ's human nature to be sinful. Neither the building nor the sect appealed to me, so I was not disappointed that the church was locked and I could hasten to satisfy my curiosity on something much nearer my heart, the famous yew hedge in Albury Park.

The gardens of Albury Park were laid out by the seventeenth-century diarist John Evelyn, who had planted many fine avenues of trees, most famously a yew hedge said to be a quarter of a mile long. Cobbett, like us on his way to Shere, wished to see the gardens as we did. Assuming that there must by a way through the park to Shere he simply rode up to the house and, 'pretty barefaced', he asked permission to leave at the other end of the estate. His cheek was rewarded, for not only was his request granted, but he was allowed to ride all about the park and to see the gardens, which he judged 'the prettiest in England; that is to say, that I ever saw in England'. I wished I had Cobbett's temerity, as the Pilgrims' Way would almost certainly have gone directly through the park and we, dutifully following the guidebook's instructions, were not only deflected from our route, but never saw the famous yew hedge. I learnt later that it is still there, now a row of noble trees rather than a hedge, but still a quarter of a mile long.

But this was a golden day and the absence of a yew hedge was not going to spoil it. I was so very glad we had not given up. What were a few aches and pains compared to the pleasure of this walk? Fortune showered delights on us as we crossed the sparkling Tillingbourne stream over the Chantry Bridge and arrived at Shere. (The name derives from the Saxon Schir or Essera, 'the bright one' - perhaps referring to the clarity of its river.) We had arranged - as we usually did when in doubt - to meet Barbara at 'the pub nearest the church'; in this case the fifteenth-century White Horse Inn was certainly the one.

It is one of those enchanting fifteenth-century pubs that still abound in Great Britain and we were once more thrown back into the past as we sat in the Pilgrims' Bar (it really does bear that name) reading of previous visitors to the inn, like the diarist Samuel Pepys, the painter Augustus John and the writer J. M. Barrie. Looking round this pretty, rather over-civilized village I found it hard to believe that this was once one of the wildest parts of Surrey and a centre for sheep stealers, brigands and smugglers. In fact smuggled brandy dating from 1720 had been found in the cellars below us.

But to a walker, the most touching thing in this delightful pub was the discovery, during recent alterations, of a pair of Elizabethan shoes found in a wattle and daub wall; in those days building a pair of used shoes into the walls was thought to bring good luck to anyone living in the house. Shoes have been thought to denote liberty - presumably because they enabled one to walk on rough surfaces and thus to travel farther, to be symbols of the female sex organ, as perhaps in the story of Cinderella, and to represent the humble and the despised.

None of this symbolism concerned me very much at the time; shoes were so important, so basic to comfort and even safety, that I would rather have ranked them with the foundations of a house. I had spent £100 on a pair of Mephisto shoes for this pilgrimage and though at the time I winced at the price, as I walked I never regretted a penny. However much the rest of my body might rebel at the constant exercise, my feet put up only the mildest protest, sometimes a little hot, a little weary, but nothing worse. I had witnessed too, the extreme discomfort that Jane had experienced through having a pair that did not fit properly. Shoes were fundamental to our present way of life and to our chances of reaching our destination. They are to a walker as a pen (or a word processor) is to a writer, a spade to a gardener, a wheel to a potter. So the idea that, even hidden in a wall, they should bring good luck, came as no surprise. That to travel barefoot was, in the Middle Ages, considered especially virtuous simply highlights their importance. Good shoes are the *sine qua non* of pilgrimage.

St James' Church, which we could just see from the pub, was completed in its present form in 1190, so the first pilgrims to Canterbury would have seen it rising from the ground. Many pilgrims had scratched crosses and dials on the Norman stonework of the south door and one of those making the journey a few years later must have lost the top of his staff, a charming bronze Madonna and Child, for it was found in 1886 by a girl out walking with her dog in the woods above Shere and can now be seen in the church.

Like the church at Compton, St James' can boast of its anchorite – a quatrefoil aperture and a squint once opened onto her cell – but some letters concerning her enclosure make one wonder if her incarceration was entirely voluntary. In 1329, wishing 'to vow herself solemnly to continence and perpetual chastity', she appears to have applied for perpetual enclosure and to have been given the consent she sought. Within two years she had returned to the world, only to beg to be enclosed again. The tone of the letter confirming her re-enclosure suggests that she was under considerable pressure to return to her tiny cell – possibly to have a resident anchorite was good for the church's reputation. The unfortunate girl was to be 'thrust back' into enclosure; she must learn 'how nefarious was her committed sin' in leaving a way of life that her judges had never tried for themselves; there was a suggestion that if she did not do as she was told she would be excommunicated.

Once again I was loath to leave ~ it seemed a day when only curiosity about the next stage of the journey could nudge me away from the content of the immediate moment; present and future were in graceful harmony. So indeed were the three of us beginning to find a harmony in our walking. Or perhaps I should say that I, the tallest and thus the fastest walker, was learning to slow down a little. Though not convinced it was a lesson I had learned completely ~ it was all too probable that, like a dog off the lead, I would streak ahead again ~ for the moment I was not going to think about that, rather I would enjoy this new serenity.

Just over a mile and we were in Abinger Hammer, where the discovery of Mesolithic pit-dwellings, inhabited by hunters some seven thousand years ago, have led to this being called the oldest village in England, though its age is attested in no other way. We had hoped to see the smith strike the hour on the famous clock, but had just missed two o'clock and did not intend to wait for the next hour, so we turned into Hackhurst Lane and were on the heathland of Abinger Roughs. I was delighted to come across a flock of Soay sheep, one of the most primitive and rugged of all surviving sheep. A notice told us that the wool should be plucked by hand or allowed to fall to the ground. These tough nonconformists come from the island of St Kilda, in the Outer Hebrides, where up to eighty years ago the young boys, as a rite of initiation, had to stand on the edge of a steep cliff and touch their toes. Those who did not fall off could claim to be men. It was curiously touching to see these independent little animals so far from their rocky, rigorous home.

The heathland, the sun, the light wind and the charm of the day again tempted us to stop and stretch out on the heath for a while. We chose as our resting place the open grassy area marked by a noble granite cross, the Wilberforce Monument, where Bishop Samuel Wilberforce, the son of the Member of Parliament who devoted his life to the abolition of the slave trade, was killed by falling from his horse. It says something for the luminosity of this day that though my notes remind me yet again of the agony in my back I have no recollection of aches and pains, just sheer delight in my surroundings. And, after a few moments, amusement at seeing a couple emerging sheepishly from one of the farm buildings opposite us, brushing the straw off their clothes and trying to look as if they had been admiring its architectural interest.

Refreshed, we skirted Deerleap Wood and rejoined the North Downs Way. Frequently the choice of paths was confusing; there were those marked on the Ordnance Survey Map - the Pilgrims' Way, one simply called 'Trackway' and the North Downs Way; there was the route preferred by Hilaire Belloc and the variations used by our guidebook. Sometimes the various routes coincided, sometimes they differed, most often because common land had fallen into private ownership, sometimes because of the interruption of modern roads, sometimes for no apparent reason. Now, from Deerleap Wood to just north of Dorking, Belloc's route, the Trackway, the Pilgrims' Way and the guidebook all sang with one voice, only the North Downs Way wheeling off to the north; it was strangely in keeping with the harmony of the day that this should be so.

So we were swept gently along the contour of the hills, passing Ranmore Common and into Denbies Coach Road, once an approach to a now demolished nineteenth-century house known as Denbies. Walking up this quiet, once baronial, drive is an experience of contrasts. The procession of yew trees - for Belloc a proof that this is indeed the Pilgrims' Way - casts a shadowy gloom along it, yet sometimes the curtains are drawn and shafts of light illumine the darkness. And as light and dark gave way to each other, so too my imagination was simultaneously peopled by wealthy visitors to the great house, driven in grand Victorian carriages, and footsore pilgrims trudging to Canterbury. The sense of forgotten grandeur is enhanced by the vegetation along the road edges, an indiscriminate mixture of wild flowers jostling with shrubs - spiraeas, deutzias, buddleias - whose ancestors must have been planted in the long-demolished gardens.

The road continues into Dorking and out along the A24, so we left all recommended routes and wound our way round the country lanes. And we were right, for when we were forced to join the highroad it was, as we had anticipated, busy, noisy and smelly; we had made a good exchange. And we had the bonus of walking through Denbies, the largest privately owned vineyard in Europe. I learnt later that the owner had made his money through what is now politely called 'water purification' but which most of us know as sewage; he then bought the vast vineyard with the wealth he had acquired, no doubt influenced by knowing that the Romans had grown grapes there 2000 years ago.

Almost hypnotized by the regularity of the stakes, weaving patterns across the fields, passing vines too young too have attained their mature gnarled knobbiness and wondering how they could possibly be ripe enough to harvest before our brief summer was ended, we walked in what we hoped was the right direction, by then very tired and looking forward to reaching our destination. Perhaps it was exhaustion, perhaps it was the serenity of the day, I don't know, but I found myself powerfully assailed by the knowledge that my husband John was looking after me. He was not just in my mind, he was somewhere up there, in benevolent and loving control. It was both infinitely sad and curiously reassuring and reminded me of a conversation just before I left home.

It was about how man relates to the saints and started when I admitted to Father David Forrester, the Chaplain of Oxford University, that I had no personal relationship with any of them and did not see much point in trying to. Perhaps it is because of my Anglican upbringing that, as the idea of indulgences does not resonate for me, neither is devotion to the saints a significant part of my spiritual life. I am very drawn to some of them - I find Teresa of Avila such an entrancing woman that I had recently written a biography of her – but it does not occur to me to talk to her or to ask her to intercede for me. And as for hoping that St Antony of Padua will find my spectacles, that St Blaise will cure my sore throat, that St Magnus of Fussen will protect the crops against vermin, that in a really desperate situation I need only turn to St Jude – it seems to me to be mildly insulting to good and devout people to waste their time on such trifling affairs. In any case, whose side are they on? If I want a sunny day for a picnic and the local farmer needs rain, whose prayer should the saint answer?

Father David was looking increasingly shocked and dismayed as I made these admissions – he must have perceived them almost as blasphemy and was clearly searching for a way to knock some sense into my head. Eventually he said, 'Don't you ever talk to John?' I said yes, rather guardedly, wondering what this admission would trap me into. 'Well, you see, it's just the same. You talk to the saints because you know them and love them.' I didn't see. It was one thing to talk to a beloved husband who was no longer there, quite another to talk to someone you had never met. Then suddenly, in the middle of Denbies Vineyard, I began to see what he had meant. It involved the whole question of how one relates to the dead; of having a theology of heaven; of crossing the barrier – the 'thin veil' – that divides the living from the dead. Where are they? Do they have any bodily form? Are they still growing, changing, developing? I did not know the answer to any of these questions, but feeling that John was somewhere 'up there', in the same realm as the saints, and that I could relate to him, talk to him, feel not only love for him but still loved *by* him, opened the way to some sort of relationship with men and women given special status by the Church. I began to see what Father David had meant.

I was so lost in these thoughts that I hardly realized how far we had walked along the A24. We arrived at the Stepping Stones pub and a long cool bitter shandy brought an end to a wonderful day's walking.

THE STEPPING STONES

Chapter Nine

The Stepping Stones
to Merstham

Another kind of pilgrimage

The Stepping Stones pub, where we had collapsed in happy
exhaustion the evening before, is named after one of the
most charming ways of crossing water that can be imagined
~ a line of small round concrete blocks, set a few inches above
water level in a gentle curve across the river, a walnut tree on
one side, a chestnut tree on the other. Not the sort of addition
to the countryside one would normally associate with a Home
Secretary, yet when they were erected in 1946 it was Chuter
Ede, who held that post, who footed the bill. They are thought
to have replaced stones that have enabled travellers to cross
the river Mole at that point for many years, so I was surprised
that neither Belloc nor Mrs Adie makes any mention of them.
Some have argued in favour of crossing the Mole a little to
the north, at Burford Bridge, but it adds a mile and a half to
the journey and in any case since the judicious placing of the
stepping stones it is an unnecessary detour. The Georgian
house that is now the Burford Bridge Hotel has its own claim
to fame; it was once a small roadside inn, whose guests
included Lord Nelson and Keats, who wrote part of *Endymion*
there. Nearby is Flint Cottage, once the home of the poet and
novelist George Meredith and visited by his friends Max
Beerbohm and J. M. Barrie.

Drawn by the River Mole just as we had been by the Itchen,
it was the stepping stones we chose. There is always something
magical·about crossing water and I had been looking forward
to this moment, so when we arrived quite early in the

morning, it was a little deflating to find several small boys exercising a dog and a radio controlled boat, the one chasing the other round and round the river. I had a ridiculous desire for the crossing to be a quiet little ritual, so waited till the dog was exhausted (or the boat's battery spent) before setting foot on the first stone. I was aware of an apprehension similar to the moment when I walked St Catherine's maze. It was, however, entirely uneventful and I was rather glad. Somehow I wanted the maze (any maze, not just St Catherine's) to retain its mysterious secrets, not to be found too readily elsewhere.

Now at the foot of Box Hill, we expected our path to lead us easily round the bottom of the hill. It could have done, perhaps it should have done, but we managed to miss the way and found ourselves set on a course that was to take us 700 feet up, to the very top. Thus I did not see two things about which I had read. One was another suggestion of Bunyan's presence in these parts – a sign to 'Doubting Castle' – though there is no mention of a castle to be found. The other was the grave of an eccentric and very rich resident of Dorking. At his death in 1800 instructions were found that he should lie on Box Hill close to his fortune, which he hoped to enjoy in the next world. He further insisted on being buried head downwards, so that when the trumpet sounds at the Last Day and the world (as he was sure it would) turned upside down, he would be the right way up and have a head start into heaven.

Taking the wrong turn was a happy mistake, for though it was a hard climb, we were fresh, the morning bright and the views alone would have encouraged us to take that route. At one point we looked back on the rolling acres of Denbies Vineyard; at another we saw such a stretch of country to the south that the sizeable town of Dorking was a mere blur of houses among the trees. At intervals we glimpsed the great expanse of the Weald, once covered by the forest of Andredesweald, and as we approached Reigate the Buckland Hills, Juniper Hill and Colley Hill, stretched before us, the one gracefully giving way to the other so that it was hard to determine where one ended and the other began.

Another bonus was that this was a Saturday, a day when more people were free to enjoy the countryside. Though usually among those who delight in having a piece of countryside to myself, after several days of isolated stretches there was a real pleasure in what one might call The Companionship of the Way. We compared notes with experienced rucksacked walkers, who pointed out bugle orchids and told us of the terrain ahead; we commiserated with a young group who had set out ill-prepared and turned back saying sadly, 'We don't even have any water'; we asked the way from a man with an orange beard and a grasping face reminiscent of a character from Dickens; we congratulated others for the distance they had covered and boasted that we were walking all the way to Canterbury; often we just waved and smiled.

All of us, in different ways, were temporarily free of our usual roles and, sharing in this liminal state, we were more ourselves, less inhibited by social pressures than usual and relating to each other in a delightfully natural way. Anthropologists use the latin word *communitas* to define this immediate, spontaneous state, a state which can only emerge in the absence of social structures, but while I appreciated this freedom and ease I take the liberty of disagreeing with one anthropologist who writes, 'The achievement of *communitas* is the pilgrim's fundamental motivation.'[1] Pilgrimage may indeed lead to *communitas*, it was one of the things I had hoped for, but a true pilgrimage is about much more.

It was good to find this state defined, as there were ways in which I was confused by my attitude to other people, both known and unknown, as I walked. I wanted to be near people, but sometimes I needed space, wanted to be able to walk at my own pace, stopping when I chose, keeping a rhythmic continuity when that was my mood. This was selfishness, of course, a microcosm of the tension between the need for company and the need for solitude most of us feel much of the time. We had intended to have long periods walking in companionable silence, but somehow this did not happen very often. We might need to consult the guidebook, someone would make a remark that turned into a conversation, often we just felt like chatting.

People have sometimes asked what I thought about when we were silent or if I was walking alone. I'm afraid the answer is that most of the time my mind was the same jumble of distractions as it usually is, prosaic, mundane thoughts chasing each other round my head. But sometimes I would pray with a sort of 'walking mantra' and, looking back, wish I had done so more often. It might be the Jesus Prayer, 'Lord Jesus Christ, Son of the living God, have mercy on me, a sinner.' Or 'Glory be to the Father, and to the Son, and to the Holy Ghost.' Once, when my back was really excruciatingly painful, it was a phrase from Psalm 91 – 'There shall no evil befall thee, neither shall any plague come nigh thy dwelling.' This day, on Box Hill, words from another Psalm came unbidden to my mind. 'Behold, how good and pleasant it is for brethren to dwell together in unity!' I was walking alone at the time and could not help smiling wryly, even as I repeated the phrase. Why should I be thinking these elevated thoughts as soon as I was NOT with my companions? I consoled myself by thinking that perhaps one can only reflect in this sort of way by oneself; that silence and solitude, or at least a measure of 'apartness', is necessary to appreciate friendship; that when actually with people one is reacting, involved rather than contemplating.

I did not totally convince myself and was still struggling with these thoughts when I remembered these words, once again from Thomas Merton: 'Go into the desert not to escape other men but in order to find them in God.'[2] So even if my motivation had been suspect – possibly I did want a temporary escape from my companions – the fruits of my aloneness were good. I was only partly reassured.

Our driver, not surprisingly, was finding coping with Pathfinder Maps at two and a half inches to a mile a bit hard, so we made a detour to the National Trust Centre to buy her a road map, then, at about 12.30, stopped at Betchworth Chalk Quarry, surrounded, surprisingly, by buddleias. We stretched out on the chalk downs high above the vast gleaming quarry, our view over the Weald partially obscured by an enormous ivy-clad tower, presumably once something to do with the work of quarrying. For a while we looked down on an army of brightly coloured skips and lorries, hidden from all but us, waiting to carry their white loads. We drank our boxes of orange juice, chatting gently as we searched for - and eventually saw in the far distance - the sails of an eighteenth-century windmill on Reigate Heath.

Sean Jennett starts his book *The Pilgrims' Way* with the arresting phrase 'Chalk is king'.[3] More and more I came to see what he meant as we passed chalk quarries such as Betchworth, where for centuries chalk has been dug and carried along the Old Road. We walked on chalk, caught its brightness shining across valleys and through woods, delighted in the gentle outlines, the steep escarpments, of the hills it forms. Chalk is soft, yet it conceals bands of flint, harder than steel, whose use for tools was discovered by primitive man. Later the Romans used it for the foundation of their roads, burning it to produce lime for cement. Chalk nourishes the yew tree, the beech and the holly, cakes our boots, gives a special clarity to the streams it carries and, at Dover, gladdens the heart of any homecoming patriot. I feel at home on chalk.

Climbing to the top of Box Hill meant we were late and we knew of nowhere on the route to have lunch before reaching the pub on which we had agreed. So it was after 2.30 in the afternoon before we approached our chosen resting place; by then we were hungry and wondering anxiously when they stopped serving lunch. I knew it was on Reigate Hill, the A217, so for once we were happy to find ourselves on metalled roads and nearing the hope of food. Thinking it was some way down the road, I asked a friendly group of walkers the way to the A217. Imagine our delight when they said, 'Just there, by The Yew Tree pub.' The very pub we were looking for ~ and it was open and serving 'Bites and Pieces', the most delectable mixture of Lincolnshire baby sausages, Chicken Tikka and 'Wings of Fire' ~ spicy chicken wings. We were surprised that often, despite the exercise, we were not very hungry at lunch time, but on this occasion we could hardly stop ordering more and more plates of 'Bites and Pieces'.

Hunger assuaged, there followed an incident of which I am ashamed, but it was important and in the interests of honesty should perhaps be told. After lunch one of my companions went to telephone her husband and came back saying to another in a 'we-wives-together' sort of way, 'There's a phone over there, by the garage.' I should say that normally I was not put out by my married friends phoning home, in fact I enjoyed the exchange of news and had not previously been even remotely touched by jealousy. But on this occasion, for no particular reason, it was too much. I knew they meant no harm at all and will be horrified to read this, but the knowledge that I could not ring John suddenly struck me with such excruciating pain that I beat a hasty retreat to the 'Ladies', where I howled ~ long, without control and, I'm afraid, noisily. Eventually I heard a voice say, 'Are you all right?' as people do. And as people do I lied, 'Yes, thank you.' She then said, 'It'll pass, I've been there.' Ordinary words, but I was comforted and I hope perhaps that kind lady reads these lines.

I'm not sure why this incident struck so forcefully. I was all too familiar with the way the pain of loss can suddenly erupt, for little immediate reason and with little warning. I had long stopped wondering at the tiny things that can provoke an overwhelming explosion. But there was something about this particular loss of control that was so complete that it was a sort of purging. Afterwards I was exhausted in the way only an emotional outburst can bring exhaustion, but it was as if

I had reached another milestone in the journey towards acceptance, the pilgrimage that follows bereavement.

It was well after 4 o'clock before we were off again. We were passing north of Reigate, halfway along our route, and wonder at the countryside through which we were passing, thoughts on such subjects as solitude and bereavement, gave way to remembering again the goal of our pilgrimage, temporarily forgotten in the moment-by-moment experience of the walk – the shrine of Thomas Becket.

Reigate remembers Becket. It would have given hospitality to pilgrims, who worshipped at a chapel in the main street named for him. It was violated at the Reformation, later demolished and an eighteenth-century market house now stands on the site. But the significance of Reigate lies also in the speculation over its name. In the Domesday Book it was known as Cherchefell, then Crechesfeld, it was not until late in the twelfth century, soon after Becket's murder, that it became Reigat or Regat, though the reason for the change is not confidently known. According to Jennett 'The first syllable may come from Saxon *raege*, the female of the roe deer, and, "gate" may be a gate as commonly understood, or be from the Icelandic, where it would mean a pass or path.[4] Hence 'the place through which the roe deer pass'.

There does not seem to be any strong reason to change the town's name to honour the activity of the local deer, so another argument, relevant to its position on the Pilgrim's Way, must be taken seriously, though it has to be admitted that it does not have scholarly approval. This suggestion has been made by Christopher Martin, an Anglican clergyman born and brought up in Reigate, who spent some time researching local documents for a paper he delivered to the Reigate Church Society and which was subsequently published in *The Times*.[5] His argument is that Henry II went to Canterbury in 1172, *before* (not, as generally claimed, after) going to Ireland and that the word derives from the Norman French, meaning 'the

King passed through'. While scholars are united in affirming that the King did not make his penitential journey to Becket's shrine until 1174, Christopher Martin did find some documentary evidence to support his claim. First was a bill for four shillings, dated soon after 1171, showing that the King and his retinue had spent a night in Winchester. Though this does not of course prove he went on to Canterbury, Martin supports that claim with another document with the words 'Iter corraedio repuit' – 'He snatched his journey in a two-wheeler'. The King could have reached Canterbury in four days, but was that indeed where he was travelling? He was so unpopular after Becket's murder that Martin argues he would hardly have gone to London; perhaps he was indeed making for Canterbury, perhaps too he stayed in Reigate with his half-brother, to whom he had given a castle. The evidence may be slight, the claim controversial, but the conclusion is satisfying, lending substance to the belief that the pilgrims did indeed travel along this way, following Henry's footsteps.

We soon reached Gatton Park, now home to the Royal Alexandra and Albert School for Deprived and Erring Children, some of whom directed us most charmingly to the church. As we passed the lake, still and mysterious behind a curtain of trees, the sky darkened dramatically and, as if sensing that something untoward was up in the cosmos, the cows streamed purposefully across the field towards what sanctuary I am not sure. My emotional crisis had blown its course, at least for the moment, and, once again walking apart from my companions, I experienced moments of sheer ecstasy. As with all such moments there is nothing more that can be said, no particular insight or explanation, but it was probably significant that I was feeling physically better than I had all week; walking was a springing delight with which even my back seemed willing to co-operate painlessly.

The village of Gatton, a manor house, a church and a few cottages, had, until the Reform Act of 1832, the ridiculous privilege of sending two Members to Parliament, and at that by appointment rather than election. Thus Gatton earned the scorn of the apoplectic Cobbett, who dubbed it 'a very rascally spot of earth', and considered it, together with Reigate, 'one rotten borough, one of the most rotten too, and with another still more rotten up upon the hill'. Ironically the Reform Act, righting this political injustice, came into being just two years after these words were published. Had Cobbett been writing a few years later he might have been better disposed towards the unfortunate object of his scorn.

For us it was another of those days when fortune smiled upon us and we were disposed to think well of Gatton. We left it to continue along the North Downs Way, passing Rupert Bowlby's nursery, from whom I had sometimes bought rare bulbs, walking through a strawberry field, once more touched that a path had been left clear for walkers, then past a gentle Saturday evening cricket match just outside Merstham.

Merstham was once a quarry village whose fine stone was used in the building of Henry VII's chapel in Westminster Abbey; it is also the place where pilgrims on their way from the Midlands to Canterbury may have joined the route. The church, whose chancel is believed to have been built with money from pilgrims, once had wall paintings of the death of Becket, and pilgrims are thought to have refreshed themselves at the wayside pool. The saint's presence was beginning to become more of a reality.

Now Merstham is a commuter town, scarred by the horrifying junction of the M23 and the M25. After a day free of motorways and modern monstrosities, this came as an unwelcome shock. Why should our quiet pilgrimage be so rudely interrupted? It is easy to fall into the trap of thinking that peace and holiness can only be found in peaceful, holy places and I was grateful to a friend who sent me a homily given during a recent pilgrimage up Croagh Patrick. The feminist theologian Angela West, told of how the peace movement of the 1980s considered which places were the most appropriate for prayer and vigil for Christians seeking peace:

> And we found ourselves going to some most unlikely places – like military bases and headquarters. From this we began to understand that as peace-seeking pilgrims in the twentieth century, we were called to the *unholy* places; the places where God is not worshipped but mocked; places where divinity is revealed by its absence – like the site of Jesus' crucifixion, hardly a holy place in the ordinary sense. And so, with rites and vigils and prayers – the tools of our tradition so to speak – we marked the spots where bombs were kept, where plans were made to destroy creation.

The paradoxical wisdom of this woke me from my bucolic dreams. I knew she was right, knew that we must not limit our search for God to places of beauty where he could so easily be recognized. It was a timely thought, for we were to spend several days far too near the roar of the M25 for any ordinary sort of comfort.

Just as we had so unexpectedly come across our lunch-time pub, so we were to be lucky at the end of the day. We came into Merstham as the sun sank over the yard-arm, looking forward to a drink and fearing that the pub where we had arranged to meet our driver would be on the other side of the A23 that now roars through the village. Again our luck was in – there was The Feathers, just across the road, and soon Barbara joined us. This time we drove a few miles ahead of ourselves, to Oxted, where we had arranged to spend two nights in one of the most delightful of our 'bed and breakfast' stops, one much frequented by pilgrims and walkers. Jenny and Tony Snell greeted us warmly and soon we were at an excellent Indian restaurant, eating one of the best vegetable Kormas I have ever tasted.

HELIX POMATIA

Chapter Ten

Merstham to Oxted

Stormy weather

'To travel properly', said that legendary traveller Dame Freya Stark, 'you have to ignore external inconveniences and surrender yourself entirely to the experience. It's no use worrying about health or time schedules. You must blend into your surroundings and accept what comes. In this way, you become part of the land and that is when the reward comes.'[1]

By this stage in the pilgrimage I knew the value of that advice – it was very similar to the words I treasured as we set out, 'Just give yourself to the pilgrimage and don't think about anything except what's going on from moment to moment.' It is, though, one thing to know the theory, another to be able to live it in practice. After two days of such pleasurable walking, this Sunday, the seventh day of our pilgrimage, was a day when little seemed to go right and I needed to feed off the wisdom of others. Though I was learning to surrender to the experience, it was hard to 'ignore external circumstances'. To try to tolerate, to accept, not to complain, seems reasonable enough, but in fact I am not sure that 'ignore' is quite the right word. After all, even yogis do not choose to sit in wet blankets, they use their extraordinary powers to dry them.

The day started badly, with my obsessive desire to walk every inch of the way creating a problem. The complications of negotiating the motorway junction led to us being dropped off at a point about half a mile farther than we had reached the night before; my companions must have been mildly irritated as I insisted on trudging back to the pub, simply in order to satisfy this obsession. It was a small point and I soon caught them up, but it made me wonder again why it was so important to me that my feet should have touched ground along the entire route. Perhaps it was quite simply that once one starts giving in to lifts, short cuts or any form of minor 'cheating' there could be no end to it. But it was a humble, even rather a petty, ambition.

An unexpected surprise lay ahead. I had read about an unusual variety of snail, *Helix Pomatia*, said to be especially good for eating and thought to have been introduced by the French at the time of the first pilgrimages. There is even the possibility that it arrived much earlier, with the Romans. It is apparently now native to this area, but the only recorded finding I had come across had been over ninety years ago. I had no idea whether they were still found in the area and had not really expected to see one when suddenly there it was, a huge white snail, the size of a small onion, gliding along the Pilgrims' Way. I could hardly believe it. My first find must have been the grandfather of them all, for we were to find ten others that morning, most of them a little smaller and a great deal more elegant, their shells a shiny chestnut brown, circled with creamy white bands. It was a living link with the pilgrims who had trodden before us, as telling as their churches, their paintings (we were only two miles from the dramatic picture of the Ladder of Salvation in Chaldon Church) or our shared path. I need hardly say we did not collect them for lunch, though we did sample some wild garlic, wondering whether it was related to the wild onions we had seen earlier and which I knew the pilgrims had gathered to supplement the scant supplies they carried with them. Perhaps they enjoyed snails in garlic sauce?

Finding these old inhabitants of the Pilgrims' Way made up in some measure for a double disappointment, first on passing The Harrow pub and finding it closed, then arriving at

Arthur's Seat. I had earmaked it early in our plans, convinced it was an ancient hill-fort, a settlement or at least a cairn. Indeed Belloc thought that there was a prehistoric camp on the southern side. So many legends surround the sixth century king that his name is associated with sites all over Britain. There are rockhollows such as Arthur's Chair, Arthur's Quoits and Arthur's Cups and Saucers; hills called Arthur's Oven, Arthur's Bed, Arthur's Hunting Seat; he has even reached the sky, the constellation of the Great Bear sometimes being known as Arthur's Wain. But here, surely a likely spot, with the Pilgrims' Way, the Trackway and the North Downs Way all uniting in one road, we searched in vain for a romantic hilltop or ancient pile of stones. Arthur's Seat, it turned out, was simply a very beautiful house. I could find no Arthurian connections, no sign of a prehistoric camp. But it had a quality of magic, and surely Druids once danced round that circle laid out on the lawn.

By noon we had reached the top of Gravelly Hill, where we rested for a while in a meadow area covered with buttercups and daisies, the staggering view marred only, as so often, by the M25. The sky was darkening and as we left the rain began to fall. Soon it was pouring down and though my Paramo jacket and overtrousers kept me dry, it was miserable walking. Worse, for reasons I cannot now remember, we had brought nothing to eat and knew of no pub for miles. Eventually I saw a parked car - the rain was too heavy even for comfortable motoring - and asked the driver where the nearest pub was. He told us there was one six miles ahead, another a mile and a half off our route. He must have seen our dismay, for he offered us a lift and I heard myself say pompously, 'It's very kind of you, but no thank you. We are puristic pilgrims.' So on we went, barely able to see, let alone appreciate, places whose names had evoked eager anticipation. Through the rain we glimpsed the Pilgrim Fort, just able to see that it was not an ancient stone building, but overgrown earthworks in the middle of a wood; we passed shapes that must have been the

Devil's Hole, Winders Hill and Hanging Wood, though they were almost invisible behind a curtain of water.

As we continued in the pouring rain for some two hours, I wondered yet again why we were doing this. Was it the challenge of a long walk? Devotion to Becket? I became so dejected that I even wondered if it was sheer masochism. I knew it was none of these things, nor could I claim to be walking for peace, in reparation or in penitence, much though I admired those who did. But when I remembered that my wish to find out how the outer, physical pilgrimage affected the inner journey the misery of being wet and hungry found its place. Sometimes one just simply has to keep going. If the weather is bad, the going rough or the next two miles nothing but boring tarmac, you cannot simply avoid it, any more than you can decide you don't much like the thought of the next two years of your life and skip it. I remember after my husband died receiving a bit of advice from Cicely Saunders, who knows as much about bereavement as anyone. As so often real wisdom needs few words; she just said, with infinite compassion, 'Plod on.' I valued these two words deeply and often remembered them, for what else can one do? And so on pilgrimage. It rains – plod on. The hill is steep – plod on. You're bored – plod on. All situations which have their inner parallels.

The anthropologist Victor Turner has some good things to say about pilgrimage as ordeal. He argues that if mysticism is an interior pilgrimage, then pilgrimage is exteriorized mysticism. Thus a pilgrim is an initiand, entering into a new, deep level of existence. I began to see how right he was. I did feel that we were living at a deeper level than usual, though I was not sure how, nor did I feel a great need to understand or to articulate the experience. If I may put my experience in rather elevated company, it was like Keats, writing about what he calls 'negative capability', when a man 'is capable of remaining in doubts, hesitations and uncertainties, without any irritable reaching out after fact or certainty'. For the moment doubts, hesitations and uncertainties were my friends and I was enjoying their company.

Eventually the birds, who always seem the first to know when rain has run its course, began to sing tentatively and I found myself humming the last movement of Beethoven's Pastoral Symphony – the one he calls 'Thanksgiving after the Storm'. And thankful we were, as the sun dried us off and I could examine my camera and notebook to see how they had survived. I was glad that we had experienced this downpour. So far the weather had been too gentle, made too few demands on us. If we were to be real pilgrims, we had to face some discomfort from the elements.

Now the countryside was washed clean, the air clear, the colours of bluebells, yellow dead nettle, white cow parsley, pink campion, refreshed and revitalized. I wish I could have said that I was refreshed and revitalized, but at least we were approaching Oxted, our goal for the day, and soon we were walking through Titsey Plantation, part of a 4000-acre estate where half a million trees were planted in the first half of the nineteenth century. I was not at all sure how we were going to cross Titsey Park, which lay beyond the plantation, as the path used by earlier pilgrims was closed to the public many years ago and there is no longer a right-of-way. We had tried to work out the various options with the help of maps and guidebooks, but were no wiser and had hoped that, once there, the route would be obvious. It was not, and I decided not to think about it until the next morning, but once again the thought of maps filled me with confusion.

I have very contradictory feelings about maps. It seems the world is divided between those who hate them and those who love them, collect them, pore over them. I remember my mother, in her nineties, asking for a World Atlas for Christmas so that she could trace the journeys she was no longer able to make. Preparing for the walk, maps had been useful, even exciting; I knew that when I returned home I would value them as reminders of the ground we had travelled. I knew too that there were times when we needed them, relied on them and I was grateful to the meticulous care of the cartographers. But there were many occasions when I found them instrusive, alien, distracting. A clerihew written by the inventor of clerihews himself, Edmund Clerihew Bentley, gives a clue:

> The art of Biography
> Is different from Geography.
> Geography is about maps,
> But Biography is about chaps.

My last twelve years had been spent writing biography; my worst subject at school was geography. Perhaps maps and I were just incompatible. But I think there was more to it than that; I think it was something to do with my desire to experience every moment, to 'blend into my surroundings' as Dame Freya Stark advocates, to banish the 'left brain' in favour of intuition, imagination, wonder. I know all too well how easy it is for the left brain to surface, to make clamouring demands on linear thinking, to pigeon-hole experience and demand factual evidence. Maps began to represent a side of myself I did not want to encourage, making me feel physically sick when I was forced to consult them. They took me out of the present moment, away from the small piece of land on which I stood, the sweep of the countryside I could see with my own eyes, into the realms of theory, where poetry was banished and irritation took its place.

I was indulging these feelings of irritation as we circled Titsey Plantation, when suddenly we heard unexpected sounds from behind the trees, though we could see nothing. A man's voice was saying prayers, a group of young voices singing hymns – in the middle of a wood . . . I was still too deaf to hear it well, but my companions assured me that it was a very pleasant sound. Later, we were to discover what was happening.

As we did not intend to negotiate Titsey Hill that evening, we deviated slightly from the route to return to the Snells in

Oxted. This self-imposed detour made me appreciate the effort involved in the detours the early travellers would have made. I had often read of pilgrims 'dropping down' from the route. For instance at Waverley Abbey, where they left the route to find food and water or to stay the night, or at Compton, to worship at the church, at Chaldon, to gaze fearfully at the mural depicting the soul's passage to heaven or hell. It seemed easy enough in theory, just a mile or so, but at the end of a long day's walking it is a different matter. I shall never forget that last stretch of road, stumbling along Bluehouse Lane into Oxted, exhausted, literally doubled up with the spasm in my back, wondering if the ordeal would ever end. Never again would I underestimate the effort made by medieval pilgrims as they 'dropped down' from their route to find accommodation, food and water or to visit a nearby shrine.

Though our day's walking was over, our day was not. We discovered that the local priest was disappointed that we were not staying with him ~ apparently pilgrims usually did ~ and that he had offered to give us communion if we went along to the church immediately. I remembered going to Mass when I had come to 'recce' an earlier stretch of the route and how I had felt bound to those who had trodden the path before me with hoops of steel. The young, the old, the disabled, the fit, gathered round the archetypal figure of the priest at the altar as they would have done all those years ago. The same sacred, unfathomable mysteries played out in modern dress. I remembered too, how Thomas à Kempis put pilgrimage firmly in its place:

> Many make pilgrimages to various places to visit the relics of the Saints, wondering at the story of their lives and the splendour of their shrines; they view and venerate their bones, covered with silks and gold. But here on the Altar are You Yourself, my God, the Holy of Holies, Creator of men and Lord of Angels![2]

So though I did not know where to find the energy, I knew I had to go, particularly as we had not been able to go to Mass in the morning. It was to be a very different experience.

The priest was very busy and could only spare a short time, so it was not a full celebration, just a few prayers and the giving of communion. As we chatted to him we discovered the answer to the mysterious singing we had overheard in Titsey Plantation. It was a healing service for animals and we learnt that it was the priest's voice that we had heard saying prayers and that a group of schoolchildren were singing the hymn. His patients had included a sick pigeon, a lame dog and a goat with a mysterious skin disease.

We moved to four chairs in the sanctuary and the priest said, 'I believe that two of you are Roman Catholics and two are not.' So, like schoolchildren lined up before the headmaster, we owned up. Yes, two were indeed Catholics, one an Anglican, one calls herself a 'lapsed' Catholic. In the course of this exchange the priest realized that I was having great difficulty hearing and to my surprise, though I knew the church held regular healing services, and now knew about the outdoor service for animals, he asked me how long I had been deaf and said he would anoint my ear and pray for healing. Then, asking us to pray with thanks, as if the healing had already happened, he touched my right ear with oil, which one of my companions was amused to notice was from the Body Shop. I had never received healing before and had not had time to form any preconceptions. My first reaction was to feel that this was a deep sharing with the pilgrims of the Middle Ages, seeking cures at holy shrines. I was very touched at his care and concern and wanted to be as open and receptive as I could.

I tried not to listen for an immediate change in my hearing as the priest read the Gospel and offered two of us Holy Communion, two a blessing. I should have known better, but I was outraged. I realize that, once he knew of our different denominations and given the present official ruling on the subject, there was nothing else he could do and I do not blame him personally in any way at all, but this division into the sheep and the goats brought home most shockingly the pain of division. Here were four people who had spent the last seven days in close companionship, separated when we should have been most together. Never have I been less comforted by the sacrament.

So we returned to our lodgings, too shaken even to discuss the wedge that had been driven between us. By mutual consent we did a 'pain measurement' (physical, not spiritual) to decide who was to have the first bath. I did not argue when I was considered to be in most need and sank my aching back gratefully into the steamy hot water.

Before we went out for dinner we shared a bottle of wine with the Snells and were regaled by stories of visiting pilgrims which put me to shame. One of their recent guests was a woman of 82, walking the Pilgrims' Way on her own. Another woman, also alone, was doing a sponsored ride by bicycle whenever the terrain permitted. (I did not discover what she did with her bicycle when she was forced to walk.) She carried a legend on her back saying 'Jesus keeps me going' and each night went into the pubs collecting money for her cause. A third woman never far from my mind was Rebecca Stephens, who even as we walked, was climbing Mount Everest. I heard later that one of her companions, who reached the top without oxygen, had to be brought home by the doctor - incidentally our driver's nephew - who himself had reached 26,000 feet when he suffered bad altitude sickness. As when we were reminded of the death of Captain Oates in the Antarctic, our slight sufferings were put firmly into place.

In the comfort of my room I wondered whether it was imagination or wishful thinking or miraculous cure, but wasn't my hearing just a little bit better?

THE NORTH DOWNS WAY

Chapter Eleven

Titsey Park to Otford

Into Kent

As soon as I woke I consulted my right ear. Yes, the slight improvement was still noticeable, so I celebrated by turning on my radio. It was that time in the morning when the BBC's Radio 4 allows a space in the dramas and disasters of the daily news for reflection. On this particular day someone was talking about Moses, reverence and holy ground. My attention was immediately caught. To stand on holy ground was one of the objects of our pilgrimage, yet when God called to Moses from the middle of the burning bush he said, 'Draw not nigh hither; put off thy shoes from off thy feet, for the place whereon thou standest is holy ground.' I was just reflecting on this paradox, that we should seek holy places while some are too holy even to be approached, when some words of Elizabeth Barrett Browning floated over the airwaves:

Earth's crammed with heaven,
And every common bush afire with God;
But only he who sees, takes off his shoes,
The rest sit round it and pluck blackberries . . .[1]

I was filled with a mixture of delight and shame. Delight at this beautiful expression of 'Finding God in all things'. Shame at how often I was one of those plucking blackberries; at all the occasions that could have been filled with joy and insights instead of miserable self-pity.

But more practical considerations called us; could we cross Titsey Park without a long and very steep detour up the hill and down the busy main road? We decided to take a leaf out of Cobbett's book and simply walk up to the house and ask if we could go through the grounds to the church at the other side. We reached some outbuildings, where four men were enjoying an early coffee break and were happy to talk to us. We discovered that the last member of the Gresham Leveson Gower family, to whom the house had belonged for over four hundred years, had recently died and most of the property is now run by a private charitable trust. It is soon to be open to visitors and I got the impression that this would mean that the Pilgrims' Way would once again become a right-of-way, in addition to the four-mile walk already laid out through the plantation for use by the public.

One of the men was the head gardener and had worked on the Titsey Estate since 1947, when it was a typical Victorian garden, the borders surrounded by box hedges. He is going to supervise its return to Victorian splendour, then he will retire. We were surprised by his matter-of-fact approach to this; he seemed less impressed by the romance of his horticultural life turning full circle than we were. I asked him about a spring that I had heard was known as Saint Thomas's Well, filling me with hopes of a connection with Becket, but was disappointed that he had never heard of it, though he assured us that the remains of the Roman villa were still there.

They had no objection to us walking through the grounds, so we were soon back on the Pilgrims' Way, by the Church of Saint James. There is now no trace of the original Saxon church, though the twelfth-century church known as the Pilgrims' Church occupied the site until 1775 when it was demolished. Memories of the heyday of pilgrimage are kept alive by the present church, which is dedicated to Saint James the Greater, brother of the Apostle Saint John and the patron saint of pilgrims, traditionally depicted with a scallop shell. His body was believed to have been translated to Santiago de

Compostela, still one of the world's most famous pilgrimage
shrines. I was surprised to find that Saint James' scallop shell
was sometimes drawn on the road signs saying 'Pilgrims' Way'.
An imaginative touch, but surely the road to Canterbury
should be indicated by a symbol special to Saint Thomas
Becket? There are plenty to choose from; the saint on
horseback, his mitred head between two erect swords, the
ampulla or miniature flask containing drops of the martyr's
blood (they had to be made of lead, as the sacred liquid was
thought to possess such vitality that wooden flasks would
have been split asunder); even the humble Canterbury Bell,
often stitched to the hats of pilgrims or tied to their horses's
reins.

To decorate the signposts in this way would be true to the
spirit of the Middle Ages, when every pilgrimage had its special
signs and most pilgrims wore badges showing where they had
been and proving that they had really undertaken the
pilgrimage. So the early pilgrims to Santiago collected scallop
shells, which they sewed onto their caps; presumably pride in
sporting the emblems of achievement compensated for the
cumbersome headgear. Later real cockle shells were replaced
by small lead badges in the shape of the shell. Pilgrims to
Jerusalem brought back a palm of Jericho, which was regarded
as a symbol of regeneration, of the victory of faith over sin.
Hence the word - and the surname - 'palmer', brought back
to England during the Crusades and part of the English
language by the time Chaucer was writing *The Canterbury
Tales*:

> Then people long to go on pilgrimages
> And palmers long to seek the stranger strands
> Of far-off saints, hallowed in sundry lands. [2]

The badge that pilgrims to Mont-St-Michel were entitled to
wear showed Saint Michael weighing souls at the last
judgment; the Annunciation was a popular token from

Walsingham; pilgrims to the shrine of Edward the Confessor could indicate their status with a representation of the saint's head, traditionally set on a long and once fashionable scarf-pin. The more badges a pilgrim wore, the more he could be seen to have travelled. The pilgrim in William Langland's *Piers the Ploughman* carried his bag and begging bowl:

> And souvenirs were pinned all round his hat – dozens of phials of holy oil, scallop-shells from Galicia, and emblems from Sinai. His cloak was sewn all over with devices – Holy Land crosses, cross-keys from Rome, and a St Veronica handkerchief across the front – to let everyone know how many shrines he had seen.[3]

I have to admit we did not have a single badge between us, nor did we see anyone wearing one, though they are still worn by pilgrims to Santiago de Compostela. This might be English reserve, it probably owes much to the fashion of the day, but beyond such considerations badges were worn in the Middle Ages for very practical reasons. They identified the traveller as a pilgrim and thus ensured he was protected and treated with charity, for anyone who dared molest a pilgrim stood to receive severe penalties from both secular and ecclesiastical courts. At some periods pilgrims were entitled to exemption from taxes and tolls; at others badges were thought to have magical powers and miraculous healings were attributed to them. They were not only popular but they were good business, especially as they were not only bought by genuine pilgrims.

We left Saint James' Church and turned into a quiet country lane, the rolling North Downs to our left, great expanses of the Kentish Weald on our right. On each side of the road there was a symphony of green and white, the white dead nettles, which I learnt to my delight are more poetically known as 'white archangels', greater stitchwort and endless shimmering heads, heavy with flower, of the ubiquitous cow parsley, which

I shall forever associate with this walk. Even the few butterflies were white, shining from the green verges.

We were now in Kent, though as the moment had not been marked we were deprived of the childish pleasure of placing a foot in each county saying 'I am in two places at once'. Five days walking in Surrey had shown me how much beauty remains in its quieter reaches and I had already promised myself that never again would I dismiss the county as mere commuter land. Nevertheless I had looked forward to reaching the 'Garden of England', with its hops, its cherry and apple orchards, the county where its inhabitants distinguish between the descendants of the Saxon invaders ‐ 'Kentish Men' and of the later Jutes ‐ 'Men of Kent'. (As far as I know the phrases have not yet been adapted to suit feminists.) It is a magical corner of England, a place of which I have only happy memories and pleasurable associations. I think I even had a vague idea that my back would stop hurting, once we were in Kent.

Kent occupies an area of nearly a million acres, once joined to the Continent and so close to France that Richard Church, writing only fifty years ago, reflected on 'a looming over of the geological past, so that the traffic, intercourse, modes of life that went on hundreds of thousands of years ago when there was no dividing sea *still goes on!*[4] Men of Kent, Kentish Men and incomers who are now affected by the Channel Tunnel and its consequent motorways may not share this romantic approach, but they can still enjoy the chalk downs, the luxuriant fertility, the bittersweet smell of hops, the orchards, the oast houses, now mostly converted into houses; they can rejoice in its wild flowers and insects and remember a time when Kent could boast sixteen varieties of ant and more beetles than any other part of Britain. It was also famous for its immigrant butterflies ‐ 'they have so little way to fly'. Though 'progress' has eliminated much of the wildlife, somehow the memory lingers and it is not hard to imagine what you can no longer see. Less destructible is the evidence of prehistoric man ~ but to talk of these ancient stones is to anticipate our slow progress through the county.

For the first few miles into Kent the Pilgrims' Way is a metalled road, but it is so pleasant a walk that I did not miss the softer surfaces to which we had become accustomed, in fact the steady walking was deeply refreshing. At last we were moving with the rhythmic continuity for which I had longed. There were no stiles to scramble over, no hills to climb, no need to consult maps or wonder whether we were on the right path. I no longer doubted that I was indeed a pilgrim, not a long-distance walker. There was more space for reflection, for entering into the minds of other pilgrims. But here it was not only the medieval pilgrims who were in my mind, but the early Celtic Christians, setting out to journey for God.

> They were emulating Abraham, who left his settled homeland at the command of Yahweh, and like him they made no plans but trusted that God would direct their footsteps. We are told that they even went to sea rudderless, letting the currents, the tides, and the winds take them to a destination known only to God. [5]

A destination known only to God; a journey without a goal. The thought of these Celts, rudderless on the open sea, threw into stark relief another question so often in my mind ~ which is more important, the journey or the arrival?

My instinct was still, as it had been before we set out, that it was the journey, that Robert Louis Stevenson was right when he said 'To travel hopefully is a better thing than to arrive' (especially when I remembered that the next line is 'And the true success is labour'). We may long for the still centre, we may agree with Saint Augustine that 'Our hearts are restless till they rest in Thee', but while we are on this earth our human nature is to move, through time and across distance; we age, change and develop. The physical movement of pilgrimage symbolizes purposefulness. It is an attempt to find meaning, an incarnation of the inner journey. I think this is why it was so important to me to walk the whole way and not to take lifts or skip stretches of road that do not seem very inviting. The parallels between the two journeys mean that to cheat in one carries the implication that one would be prepared to cheat in the other.

But if the journey is the more important, what of the arrival, the goal? Would I mind if I did not actually arrive at my destination? I knew that I would, that the sense of anticlimax would be terrible, but at the moment I felt I would rather fail to reach Canterbury than bypass the physical effort and travel by car.

The sacred place and the act of pilgrimage are, like all journeys and all arrivals, intertwined. There can be no Way of the Cross if there is no crucifixion; even the rudderless Celts would eventually have arrived somewhere. I began to think that perhaps journeying and arriving reflect different parts of ourselves, especially when I discovered that some people strongly resist the idea that the journey might be more important than the arrival. I liked the reaction of a friend I mentioned this to. 'Journeying', he said, 'has liberal overtones. It is in the exploration mode, agonizing, wondering, doubting and lost. As opposed to a conservative attitude, about confidence, certainty and arrival.' I liked, too, a saying of the sixth-century philosopher Boethius, which, at least for Christians, should put an end to discussion, 'Thou art the journey *and* the journey's end.'[6]

So as we walked that day there was space for fantasy, to remember that pilgrimage is a state of mind as well as an external act. Always on the move, never settled in time or place, the remorseless tramp, tramp, tramp, brought about a slightly hypnotic state, where thinking and dreaming came together in a sort of poetic wholeness. *The Pilgrim's Rune*, a Celtic poem that we sometimes read during our evening meditations, seemed to fit this mood. (Airt is a Gaelic word meaning a point of the compass.)

King of the Elements – Love-Father of Bliss,
In my pilgrimage from airt to airt,
From airt to airt,
May each evil be a good to me,
May each sorrow be a gladness to me,
And may Thy Son be my foster-brother,
Oh may Thy Son be my foster-brother.

Holy Spirit – Spirit of Light,
A pilgrim I throughout the night,
Throughout the night,
Lave my heart pure as the stars,
Lave my heart pure as the stars,
Nor fear I then the spells of evil,
The spells of evil.

Jesus – Son of the Virgin pure,
Be thou my pilgrim-staff throughout the lands,
Throughout the lands,
Thy love in all my thoughts, Thy likeness in my face,
May I heart-warm to others, and they heart-warm to
me.
For love of the love of Thee,
For love of the love of Thee.[7]

In this dreamy, heart-warming state, I had lost all interest in
our destination, content to live only in the present, but dreams
were soon put to an end by an Act of Parliament. The Pilgrims'
Way used to go across the Chevening Estate, past the
handsome mansion built by Inigo Jones. It was for two
hundred years the home of the Stanhopes and in 1780 the
third Earl Stanhope, irritated by the continual passing of
pilgrims, managed to pass an Act of Enclosure giving him the
legal right to forbid anyone to walk through his property. So
now walkers have little choice but to turn left up Sundridge
Hill – which is very steep – and wend their way through woods
and fields, keeping a discreet distance from the house and its

attendant policeman, for in 1959 the seventh Earl Stanhope gave it to the nation and Chevening is now the official home of the Foreign Secretary.

We had heard that some people risk the police and simply walk across the estate, frequently getting away with it. But trespassing did not seem to be in the spirit of pilgrimage and, less high-mindedly, I suspected that there could be guard dogs on patrol, so we resisted the temptation and set off up the hill.

I was still in a slightly dreamy state and, before I realized what was happening, I had left my companions behind and reached the point where we should turn into the woods. I sat on a log, just inside the woods, and waited. I waited so long that I began to wonder if there had been an accident and set off down the hill again. Unable to see them, I turned back and went on up, assuming they had missed the turn. Still there was not a soul in sight. I started back down again, by now hot, tired and beginning to panic. I had the guidebook and, though they had a map, they could easily have gone too far north and landed up at Knockholt. I also realized my dependence on them. It was one thing to wander off on my own, but I needed to know that my companions were near at hand. In despair I flagged down a passing car, to find that my luck was in ~ it was Barbara, our driver, on her way to our lunch-time meeting place. She set off in pursuit, eventually returning with the lost walkers looking sheepish and admitting they had been so deep in conversation that they had not seen me sitting by the road. I wondered how I could have failed to see them passing.

The detour through the woods caused by the whim of the third Earl Stanhope was so pleasant that we easily forgave him his lack of generosity. I also warmed to the thought of his daughter, 'an exquisite example of the eccentric English "milady", a type that from time to time recurs in our native manners, much to the amusement of our neighbours on the Continent'.[8] Lady Hester Stanhope had an argument with her father of such dimensions that she left home and went to London, where she acted as hostess for her uncle William Pitt.

She must have exercised more control at Downing Street than at Chevening, for when Pitt died she was given a state pension large enough to enable her to take off again, this time to the Lebanon, 'where her craving for domination, if not her social wit, could be exercised without restraint. She became a sort of Hippolyte among the natives, and maintained her hypnotic hold over them until her death in 1839'.[9]

When we eventually saw her childhood home we thought we must have stumbled on an important international conference, for there were scores of cars and even more official figures than we were expecting. Were they discussing Bosnia? The Middle East? South Africa? We later discovered it was none of these things. It was an antiques sale, and according to someone we later met who had been there, 'it was all junk'.

Our next stopping place was Chevening Church, dedicated to Saint Botolph, a favourite saint for travellers and pilgrims. He did not seem to favour us that day, for it was the first and only time that we failed to meet Barbara at the agreed time. What was worse there was no pub nearby. She was normally so punctual that we were beginning to worry when she turned up with four bottles of beer which by then (it was three o'clock and we had had no lunch) we needed badly. One of the patrons of the antiques sale saw our frustrated attempts to open the bottles on a stone wall and produced a bottle opener, so we sat on the grass verge, the graves of the Stanhopes in the churchyard behind us, drinking gratefully as we watched the expensive cars rolling out of the drive of Chevening House. It was after four o'clock before we set out on the road to Otford, apprehensively, for we knew it was a busy road and the rush hour was approaching.

It was worse than we had feared. We not only had to find our way across the M25, but had to walk for some way down an extremely busy, narrow road with neither verge nor pavement. Blinded and confused by traffic, we missed the diversion to the hamlet of Twitton that would have given us a little peace, eventually reaching the outskirts of Otford, relieved that we had arrived in one piece. It's all very well to say that ordeal is part of pilgrimage, but roads like this are a danger not only to the walker, but to drivers, doing their best not to hit us. I appreciated more than ever the efforts of groups like the Ramblers' Association to keep footpaths clear for walkers.

Once through the traffic and sprawling urbanization of the outskirts of Otford, the centre of the village, with its old cottages, the church, the old pubs and the village green and willow-shaded pond, is delightful. But its ancient glory is long since departed. When the Domesday Book was compiled Otford boasted a hundred small farms and six mills; by the Middle Ages an estate presented to the Church at Canterbury had become one of the largest properties owned by the Archbishops. Kings travelling from Greenwich and heading for the coast passed through Otford and in 1520 Henry VIII, with Queen Catherine of Aragon and a retinue of some 5,000, stayed here on their way to the Field of the Cloth of Gold.

Otford also has many associations with Thomas Becket. Just off the green stands a ruined octagonal tower, part of the palace built by one of his successors and finished just in time to fall into King Henry's hands at the dissolution of the monasteries. This was the site of a previous palace much loved by Thomas Becket and where he used frequently to stay. There is a spring to the east of the palace known as Becket's Well as it is said that it was conjured forth by Becket striking the ground with his staff.

Another story about Becket is less flattering. It is told by the Elizabethan historian William Lambard, who refers to it as one of the Saint's 'spiteful miracles':

As Thomas à Becket walked on a time in the Olde Parke (busie at his prayers), that he was much hindered in devotion by the sweete note and melodie of a nightingale that sang in a bush beside him, and that therefore (in the might of his holynesse) he injoined that from

henceforth no byrde of that kynde shoulde be so bolde
as to sing thereabouts.[10]

Perhaps one should be shocked by such churlish behaviour.
I have to admit that I warm to saints when I see their feet of
clay, so find this very human irascibility rather endearing. The
more so as his command was not obeyed. As we crossed the
bridge over the railway line I heard, I promise you, the song
of a nightingale.

ST THOMAS BECKET

Chapter Twelve

'The Holy Blissful Martyr'

I n reaching Otford, only fifty miles from our destination, we were coming under the indefinable aura of the See of Canterbury. The power of the State, once wielded from Winchester, was giving way to the power of the English Church, for nearly fourteen hundred years centred at Canterbury. If this feeling belongs largely to the realms of the imagination, it was embodied in the ruins of the great archiepiscopal palaces. We had already seen what is left of the palace at Otford, we were approaching those at Wrotham and Charing. Canterbury's great Archbishop Thomas Becket had never been far from my mind but now his claims to my attention were becoming more insistent. It is time to take a break from our pilgrimage and remember something of the martyr's life.

The cult of Thomas Becket, the most celebrated in England for over two hundred years, owes its existence to a quarrel and a murder. The story would have been instilled deep into the hearts and minds of the pilgrims who trekked to his shrine; over eight hundred years later it is still enshrined in memory. Becket's cause, in essence his insistence that criminous clerics should be tried by ecclesiastical, not royal, courts, does not sit easily in today's climate and some of my questions had shocked his admirers. Did he deserve the honours that were heaped upon him? Did his fame not lie as much in the violence of his death as in the quality of his life? Had he died in his bed would his name have survived for more than a few decades? Most poignantly of all, was his cause worth dying for?

Becket is not one of today's most popular saints. Even Father David Forrester, one of his most loyal admirers, gave rather unexpected answers to my question, 'What is it that you most love about him?' 'Because he is one of the last people you would expect to be canonized, so he gives people like me hope,' he said. Then he added, 'Also because he was such a proud man and because he's a minority cause.' I was touched, but not convinced.

Becket was born in Cheapside in 1120, the son of Gilbert and Matilda Becket. Romance preceded his birth, indeed the strange tale became the subject of several popular ballads. The story is that Gilbert, when on pilgrimage to the Holy Land, was captured and reduced to slavery. In this sorry state he attracted the attention of the daughter of a Saracen chief, who fell in love with him, helped him to escape and followed him to England. Only knowing two words of English, 'London' and 'Becket', she used her first word to find a ship to take her to England, the second to find her love. Once there she ran round the city repeating 'Becket, Becket' until she had the good fortune to run into Gilbert's manservant. He took her to his master, who behaved honourably and married the faithful princess; it is romantically believed that Thomas was conceived the very next night.

Thomas received a good education with the canons of Merton Priory and at schools in London, then studied theology in Paris. There is no evidence that he intended to become a priest, though he took minor orders and some accounts say that he made a vow of chastity. When he was twenty-five his father persuaded Theobald, Archbishop of Canterbury, to receive Thomas into his household. There he found himself in the company of brilliant young men, living and working at the hub of affairs during the turbulent years of Stephen and Matilda's reign. His intelligence and charm soon made him a favourite of the ageing archbishop Theobald, who, seeing his clerk's potential, sent him to study law abroad.

Becket was the subject of at least ten biographies in the decade following his death, so we have a clear idea what he was like. He was intelligent, though no scholar, worldly yet ascetic, proud, obstinate, energetic. Above all he was loyal, had he not been he might have led an easier life. A recent biographer, Frank Barlow, has trawled through all the accounts and summarizes his appearance and character thus:

> Tall and slender, vivacious yet elegant, he was extremely good-looking in youth and handsome when older. He had fair skin and dark hair. His features were regular, although his nose was rather long and aquiline. His forehead was wide, his eyes were bright and his expression was calm and happy. It is obvious from his physical achievements in early manhood that his constitution was in essentials robust . . . He had a modest and pleasant turn of speech and engaging manners. He was prone to frivolity and ostentation in dress, enjoyed company and joined his friends in their buffooneries. He was particularly addicted to hunting and fowling.[1]

Does this sound like a saint in the making? There seems no mention of warmth or prayerfulness, no indication that he led a devout life, though his absolute truthfulness and chastity is stressed by all commentators. This claim to chastity may tally with his early vow, but it does not accord with his life-style. Perhaps his biographers wanted to cast a blind eye on his human peccadilloes and present him as the saint he was to become; perhaps, though, it was true, for sainthood does not demand a life totally free from sin and no cover-up was necessary.

He soon found favour with the future king, for in 1151, as Archdeacon of Canterbury, he was sent to Rome, where he succeeded in dissuading the Curia from sanctioning the coronation of Stephen's son Eustace, thus leaving the way clear for Henry, Matilda's son. So when Henry was crowned in 1154 it was natural that the new king should show his gratitude by appointing Becket, then 36, as his chancellor, the chief ecclesiastical servant in the royal household.

At the heart of Becket's cause was the relationship between Church and State; the violent storms that beleaguered his life were caused by his conflicting and changing loyalties from one to the other. As a member of the archbishop's household Becket had stood firmly on the side of the Church and Theobald hoped that, as chancellor, he would continue to support the privileges that had been conferred on the Church by Stephen. But personal loyalty overtook loyalty to the Church and as soon as he was appointed chancellor he became the king's man. Now both courtier and churchman, he took the king's side, identifying with his military aspirations and taxing the Church heavily to pay for Henry's foreign wars. He was a loyal and skilful servant to the king.

So too his life-style changed. As chancellor he maintained a magnificent retinue, something noted – and questioned – both at home and abroad. If the chancellor travelled in such grandeur, how splendid must the king's retinue be? He became so wealthy that he was even able to give his master three fully equipped ships. But the contradictory impulses that threaded through his life led him to give alms lavishly, to indulge in secret penances such as wearing hairshirts and, in keeping with the medieval idea that there was a connection between mortification and sanctity, having himself flogged. And apparently he remained chaste. An anonymous biographer claimed that he refused to indulge in sex even when recommended to by the doctors. Sex was not a healing medicine, the chancellor is said to have asserted, rather it was polluting to both body and soul.

Which was the true Becket, the ascetic priest or the wordly-wise careerist? It was universally agreed that his lavish life-style was to honour his master and that most of his huge expenditure was on the king's account. He was never accused of embezzlement, bribery or attempting to create a private fortune. He was in fact totally beholden to his royal master and dependent on his patronage. One of Thomas' clerks argued that his behaviour was based on expedience. His job as chancellor was to reconcile Church and State and for this a little dissimulation was necessary. Frank Barlow writes that:

> He should seem to do what he did not do, and seem not to do what he did do. Hence a series of paradoxes: in the interests of charity he often acted contrary to charity, against the law for the sake of law, against religion for religion's sake. [2]

It is also possible that paradox was rooted deep in his nature; that he was genuinely torn between loyalty to Church and State, between God and man, between worldly grandeur and monastic simplicity.

Becket's tragedy, as with so many human tragedies, was brought about by a relationship, his friendship with the young King Henry II. It was in some ways a surprising liaison. Henry was coarse, restless, lecherous and blasphemous; he was also hard-headed, courageous and shrewd. But, despite the difference in their temperaments, friends they were, both on and off duty, Becket flattered by the association with royalty, Henry respecting his chancellor's experience and intellect. Master and servant hunted, dined and gamed together - for eight years they were rarely apart. For all this period Becket put the king's wishes first, no longer favouring his previous master, Archbishop Theobald. Even so, and despite Becket's worldly life, Theobald, hoping that his former archdeacon would have some chance of influencing the king, wanted Becket to succeed him as archbishop and when he died Henry, assuming Becket would be as loyal as archbishop as he had been as chancellor, did indeed decide in his favour. It was said that the one person to doubt the wisdom of the appointment was Becket himself. Henry was confident in his choice; he would have his own man as head of the English Church.

On 2 June 1162 Becket was ordained priest and the next day, in a splendid ceremony, he was enthroned as archbishop. It was a dramatic change in his life. He was not only a new archbishop, he was a new priest, new to the saying of Mass and all other priestly duties. It also brought about a change in his loyalties. To Henry's understandable disappointment, indeed outrage, his archbishop switched his loyalty from the king to the Church. Now when the interests of Church and State conflicted he sided with the Church, and to demonstrate this beyond any shadow of doubt, he gave up the office of chancellor. He did not have the time to carry two heavy posts, in any case his position as archbishop meant that he had no need of it in career terms. Most of all he wanted to show the king that the affairs of State must be separate from the Church.

This change of priorities was reflected in a secret life, known to few during his lifetime; it was symbolized perfectly by the clothes that, some time after his enthronement, he took to wearing. To all outward appearances he was dressed as a prince of the church, but under the full-length robe was a monastic tunic, under that a hair shirt. The contradictions in his character could hardly have been more aptly demonstrated. So too did his life-style speak of two different people. He still entertained magnificently - his guests included scholars, knights and important people from every walk of life; boar, venison, pheasant and chicken were served at his table - but he himself ate moderately and the dark hours of the night saw a new dimension to his asceticism. As he himself put it, he changed from being 'a patron of play-actors and a follower of hounds, to being a shepherd of souls'.[3] Every night, around 2 a.m, he secretly stripped to his stole and hair shirt and washed the feet of thirteen poor men, giving them 4p each; he is believed to have sent food and clothing to the poor and sick and to have devoted a tithe of his revenues to the poor. Every morning he studied the Scriptures with a tutor (he recognized that as a newly ordained priest he had much to learn) and then meditated on what they had studied. He spent long hours in private devotion, continued to undergo scourgings and celebrated Mass frequently, though not daily. One of his clerks, John of Salisbury, remarking on Becket's reverence for the Mass, found he associated Becket's reverence for the sacrament with the gift of tears.

I was beginning to warm to this contradictory man. There is something touching about the fiery, obstinate archbishop practising a virtuous life in the secrecy of the night, during the day taking on all comers in defence of his cause. Indeed some writers feel that Becket's change of life-style precipitated the quarrel with the king; even if his secret was only known to few, it must have been clear that he was trying to follow the ways of God in preference to the ways of the royal court.

The cause for which Becket was to die needs to be seen in its historical context. Today we are accustomed to one law applying, at least in theory, to all men; in the twelfth century there were separate ecclesiastical and secular courts and Becket wanted it to stay that way. Henry, however, was anxious to re-establish earlier custom and to strengthen secular, as opposed to ecclesiastical, jurisdiction. There were arguments on both sides. In favour of Becket's argument that the Church should try its own offenders was that clerics (and thus most educated men in the country, for they were nearly all in the Church's service) could be protected against the power of kings and barons, who were quite ready to forget the law when it suited them. Becket felt that he was defending the Church against the abuses of secular power.

On the other hand the Church itself abused its powers and there were many cases of criminal clerics sheltering under the Church's wing, where the punishments were lighter. Some cases, in which the archbishop himself was involved, particularly infuriated Henry. For instance, when a clerk from Worcester killed a man in order to rape his daughter, Becket was able to put him in the bishop's prison, thus protecting him from the sterner punishment that would have been meted out by a secular authority.

Becket had only been archbishop for a year when Henry asked the bishops to sanction the transfer of the trial of criminous clerics to the secular courts. The following year, 1164, he set up a council to draw up a code of practice – the Constitutions of Clarendon. Among the sixteen provisions was one that declared that criminous clerics should be sent first to the king's court, and after being formally accused should, if the court so decided, be sent to the ecclesiastical court for trial, where an official would be present on behalf of the king. If found guilty the accused cleric would then be degraded and sent back to the king's court for punishment. Clerical immunity was thus threatened in two important ways – clerks were no longer to be automatically handed over to the Church and their eventual punishment would be in the secular courts, where they would not receive special treatment. Further, Becket stood firm on the principle that God himself will not judge twice for the same offence.

When the archbishop's approval was sought Becket, untypically, equivocated. He first accepted the code of practice, then refused to sign, finally completely withdrawing his assent. It was probably, writes Frank Barlow, 'the lowest point Thomas ever reached. He had let everyone down, the king, the bishops, the Church, above all himself.'[4] Becket himself was clearly deeply ashamed, for soon after the council he suspended himself from priestly duties, wrote to the pope asking for pardon and absolution and tried, unsuccessfully, to flee the country.

Church and State were now at war and Henry, enraged and disappointed in his old friend, tried to humiliate his archbishop in any way he could. He even had him tried on a number of mostly baseless charges, unrelated to the central issue. Becket refused to accept their judgment, in any case he resolutely opposed the right of the king's court to try him. The trial ended in tumult and insult, the barons reviling him and shouts of 'perjurer' and 'traitor' following him as he left the hall. But outside the crowds acclaimed him. To them Becket was a lonely figure championing the Church against oppression and cruelty. The lines were drawn, the scene set for the last stage of the drama.

Three weeks later Becket fled the country; this time Henry made no attempt to prevent him and Becket spent the next six years in exile in France. Whatever the rights and wrongs of Becket's stance he remained convinced, zealously pursuing his cause for all this period in exile. He wrote to Henry, he wrote to the pope, and as every literate person joined in this copious and often acrimonious correspondence the original issue was drowned in a sea of words. Each side brought out their heavy artillery. Henry confiscated Becket's possessions, took over his residence of Saltwood Castle, ordered the seizure of all the churches and revenues of Becket's clerks, exiled all his relations and members of his household, together with their families. Thomas issued excommunications and threatened ecclesiastical censures. Against the express command of the Pope and in a final attempt to humiliate Becket, still in exile, Henry had his son crowned, not merely as his successor but as co-regent. This was a direct blow to the prestige of the Archbishop of Canterbury, whose privilege it was to crown monarchs. Worse, the coronation was conducted by Becket's old enemy, Roger of York.

This is as much a human as a political story and both men wanted a reconciliation – at the very least it was in their own interests – and they arranged to meet in a windy field in France. The bitterness had been replaced by a weary sadness. 'Oh, why will you not do my wishes?' lamented Henry. 'All things would be put in your hands.' Becket could only reply, 'My Lord, my soul tells me you will never see me again in this life.' They parted without exchanging the kiss of peace. Becket, though well aware of the risks, decided to go home. In fact he had four weeks to live.

His arrival at Sandwich must have warmed his heart, for he was not, as he had expected, greeted by armed men, rather by a welcoming crowd running into the water shouting 'Blessed is he that cometh in the name of the Lord.' When he reached Canterbury he was greeted by music and bells and a procession of chanting monks. Becket dismounted, took off his boots and arrived at the cathedral on foot, prostrating himself and greeting each monk with the kiss of peace. He then spoke on the text from Hebrews, 'For here we have no abiding city, but we seek one to come.' On Christmas Day the contradictory elements in his nature were dramatically shown when he first preached on the text 'On earth peace to men of good will' and told the congregation that they would soon have another martyr. He then pronounced excommunication on all who had violated the rights of the Church, including specifically Ranulf de Broc, who had been responsible for implementing the king's orders in appropriating the revenues of Church property and who still held Saltwood Castle. 'May they all be damned by Jesus Christ' he is believed to have said, hurling flaming candles to the ground.

Meanwhile the final drama was unfolding in France. Several prelates joined Henry at Bayeux, complaining about Becket, fearful that he was going to arouse the country and assert the supremacy of the Church over the Crown. They incited the king perhaps even more than they intended and eventually he uttered those fateful and famous (though variously phrased) words, 'What miserable drones and traitors have I nourished and promoted in my household, who let their lord be treated with such shameful contempt by a low-born clerk!'[5] Four knights were present, Reginald FitzUrse, William de Tracy, Hugh de Morville and Richard le Bret. They interpreted his words their own way and left immediately with murder in their hearts. They travelled by separate routes for England, where they were welcomed by de Broc and spent the night of 28 December with him and his family at Saltwood. The next morning they rode the remaining fifteen miles to Canterbury, mustering support as they went. They arrived at the archbishop's palace at three in the afternoon, demanding, in the king's name, to see the archbishop.

The events of Becket's last day on earth were witnessed and chronicled by at least five people; seldom can a murder have been so publicly committed or the perpetrators so confidently known. There may be disagreement about this or that detail, about exactly what words were used, but over the broad sweep of the drama there can be no doubt.

The knights arrived to find Becket still at table, talking to members of his household. At first he pretended to ignore them, and even after acknowledging their presence he said nothing for several moments. Eventually the silence was broken by one of the knights asking if he would like to talk publicly or in private. At first Becket wanted privacy, but as soon as he saw the way the conversation was going he recalled the monks and clerks as witnesses. The knights had concocted a message from the king demanding Becket's loyalty to the young Henry, insisting that he absolve all the suspended bishops and that he should give way on everything for which he had stood for so many years. They must have known that Becket could never have agreed to their demands (would history have been different if he had, or were the knights too inflamed, too determined on their course?) and indeed he did not. He clung to his interpretation of 'Render unto Caesar the things that are Caesar's and unto God the things that are God's.'

At this the knights lost all control. They jumped to their feet, shouting, twisting their long gloves into knots, gesticulating and thrusting their heads into his face. Becket joined in the verbal abuse and the knights left yelling, 'It is you who threaten.' As they left, the archbishop followed them to the door shouting that he had not returned to Canterbury to run away. 'You will find me here. And in the Lord's battle I will fight, hand to hand, toe to toe.'

Becket knew what was coming. He had spent much of the day in prayer, calling on the saints to come to his aid; he had made his confession, assisted at Mass and three times had asked to be flogged. It is said that he had considered flight, but had decided that 'God's will be done.' Clearly his monks understood what might happen, for they urged him to seek refuge in the cathedral. When he scorned their timidity they dragged him away, through the cloisters, into the north transept of the cathedral, where Vespers had begun. Darkness was falling and it would have been easy for Becket to hide in the vast cathedral, lit only by candles, but he insisted that the door be left open and turned to await the knights. The uproar had so frightened the monks that many abandoned their prayers and hid in the aisles; terrified servants scattered through a door Beckett had ordered to be left open to allow them to escape. The archbishop was left with just three of his companions.

Soon the knights stormed into the cathedral shouting, 'Where is Becket, a traitor to the king and kingdom?' 'Here I am,' replied Becket, 'not traitor to the king, but a priest of God. What do you want of me?' The knights tried to drag him out of the cathedral so that no sacrilege should be committed, but Becket struggled and somehow stayed his ground. By now all had deserted him save Edward Grim, a visiting cleric from Cambridge. Becket stood with his back to a pillar and said, 'Into thy hands, O Lord, I commend my spirit.'

When the attack began Becket managed to fell William de Tracy, hurling him on the stone floor with torrents of abuse; FitzUrse closed in, shouting 'Strike! Strike!', but only succeeded in removing the archbishop's cap. De Tracy leapt up and struck hard, but the blow fell on the faithful Edward Grim, whose arm was cut to the bone, merely grazing the archbishop. De Tracy struck again, this time stunning Becket, who fell to the ground. Grim writes that as he fell he murmured, 'For the name of Jesus and the protection of the Church I am ready to embrace death.' The *coup de grâce* came from Richard le Bret, who struck with such violence that his sword sliced off the top of Becket's skull and shattered in two pieces on the hard floor. Finally Hugh de Horsea, a subdeacon, put his foot on his archbishop's neck, thrust his sword into the open skull and scattered blood and brains onto the floor. 'Let's be off, knights,' he said. 'This fellow won't get up again.'

Still they were not done. Shouting 'The King's Men! The King's Men!' they ransacked the palace for evidence of treason, beat the servants, and made off on stolen horses, saddlebags crammed with their spoils. They spent the night at Saltwood, at one time the residence of the man they had murdered.

Once the knights had left, the monks and clerics found the courage to attend to the body of the murdered archbishop. Blood and brains were collected and the body carried to the high altar, with bowls placed under the bier so that every drop of blood should be saved. Few of them knew about Becket's ascetic practices and they were amazed to discover the monk's habit and a hair shirt, seething with lice and worms, under the ecclesiastical robes. Frank Barlow suggests that 'It would seem that it was these revelations which converted an important section of the monks to Thomas's cause. Had his furs been of gris and vair and his underclothes of samite and silk there might easily have been no martyr.'[6] The monks were deeply impressed and burst into cries of 'Look, he's a true monk!' and 'Saint Thomas'. The eagerness to save every drop of blood intensified. Already Becket was being seen as a martyr and the townspeople crowding into the cathedral dipped their fingers into the blood and made the sign of the cross on their foreheads. Fearing that someone should try to steal his body, the monks clothed it in the consecration clothes of archbishop, together with the insignia of his office, and buried it in the crypt. There could be no funeral Mass. The church had been polluted by his murder.

Immediately the miracles began. On the very night of the murder a paralysed woman of Canterbury was cured with some of Becket's blood that her husband had wiped up on a cloth. Within days news had spread and miraculous cures were reported in Sussex, Gloucestershire and Berkshire. By Easter at least 20 miracles had been claimed and in June public acclaim had defeated official hostility and pilgrims were openly wearing ampoules of 'the water of Thomas' ~ a few drops of his blood diluted with gallons of water. A few months later news began to arrive of miracles in Germany, France, Italy and Holland. By then some of the Canterbury monks had travelled to Rome to give the Pope their version of the story and within a year legates were sent to investigate the miracles. Becket was canonized in 1173, his Feast Day being commemorated on the day of his murder, 29 December. Becket's cause was not only receiving popular support but had the official backing of the Church.

From that momentous day in 1170 until Henry VIII ravaged the shrine in 1538 pilgrims flocked from all over England and the Continent and his shrine became the most popular in England. An official register was kept of the miracles wrought by the relics of the saint (there were seven hundred recorded miracles in the fifteen years after his death) and plenary indulgences were given to those who visited the shrine. On 7 July 1220 the saint's body was translated from the crypt to the new Trinity Chapel behind the high altar, the shrine magnificently adorned with gold, silver and jewels offered by the pious. Now the saint had a second festival, in summer, a kinder time for pilgrimage. The number of pilgrims increased and the coffers of Canterbury became correspondingly richer.

The arguments for Becket's canonization rested on three planks ~ the issues for which he had fought, the manner of his death and the miracles. There are those who feel that his posthumous reputation has been exaggerated, but Frank Barlow writes that after Becket's death the Christian Church was never quite the same again.

He had, through his stand against Henry and his martyrdom, brought the archaic English customs to the notice of the pope and cardinals and all canon lawyers and had succeeded in getting them scrutinized, debated and in part abolished or reformed.[7]

Even if these changes would have happened anyway, in time, Becket's achievement was remarkable, especially considering the strength of his papal and royal opponents.

I still wonder if the support of ecclesiastical privilege deserves uncritical admiration, nor is the matter of miracles an easy subject for the twentieth-century mind. Nevertheless, writes Benedicta Ward, 'it was for them and for the martyrdom that Thomas was canonized; the evidence of a life of outstanding virtue was not in this case required or available.'[8] Even if the issue over which he fought is no longer deemed worthy of canonization, it is impossible not to admire the courage with which he fought for it and the dignity with which he died. And there is no question that he died a martyr's death.

THE COLDRUM STONES

Chapter Thirteen

Otford to
The Coldrum Stones

Pagan Bones

We spent the night in Otford, a couple of miles from the ruins of Becket's favourite palace and quite close to the bridge where I had heard the nightingale. The next morning saw one of those occasions which showed once again how pilgrimage, especially in the company of other people, can expose traits and characteristics that can often be concealed. As at Ropley Dean, on the second day of our pilgrimage, so on this day I was uneasy about having my own way and I allowed myself to be talked into a deviation which not only led to us losing our way quite seriously but resulted in a situation which shed another unexpected light on the parallel between the inner and outer pilgrimage.

It started off with the best of intentions. Our landlady knew that the direct route from Otford to Wrotham was, like the road into Otford which we had negotiated the day before, narrow, busy and without verges. She advised one of my companions to avoid the road by taking the North Downs Way. Though it sounded a lovely walk I did not want to stray so far from the Pilgrims' Way, which at this point coincided with the road; also I knew that our guidebook suggested walking along a small path running beside the road which should have been tolerably quiet. However in the face of advice from an Otford local I thought perhaps I had misunderstood the guidebook and that the road might indeed frighten one of my companions, who I had by then discovered was really scared by heavy traffic. In short I did not have the courage of my convictions.

So we set off, climbing high up to the north of the Pilgrims' Way and at first glad that we had done so, for the day was fine and the views spectacular. As we were no longer on the route suggested by the guidebook we relied on our map and the acorn markers indicating the North Downs Way, but became increasingly doubtful that we were on the right track. After about two hours we came to a main road and when we asked to be directed to Wrotham were told to go up the hill and we would soon be there. It did not feel right, but we did as we were told and walked another couple of miles, eventually reaching a small village, a signpost marking a variety of places, all unfamiliar to us except Brand's Hatch, and we knew we did not want to be there. We then realized why the 'Pathfinder' had not helped us, we had gone so far north that we were no longer on the map and had not been for some time.

We had been walking for over three hours and it was already twelve o'clock, the time we had arranged to meet Barbara in Wrotham. What should we do? There were some pretty cottages in the village and, quite at random, we rang a doorbell to ask if we could use the telephone. A benevolent spirit must have been looking after us, for a charming elderly lady, looking like someone from *Cider with Rosie*, greeted us warmly. She told us we were at West Kingsdown, that we had been misdirected and were going away from Wrotham, which was six miles in the other direction, but that she was just going there to do some shopping and would give us a lift. Delighted by her kindness and amazed by such trust in an age of muggers, we did not hesitate to accept and were soon holding half pints of bitter shandy in The Bull Inn at Wrotham.

I was distraught out of all proportion to the situation. I knew I was being pedantic to the point of lunacy, but the interruption of the continuous line from Winchester to Canterbury was like a physical wound; in fact it was worse, because it could not be healed. We had not only lost our way but we had missed several miles of the journey and short of starting all over again there was no recovering it. Our pilgrimage was scarred and mutilated. It was broken-backed.

I wondered if I should ask to be taken back to Otford and retrieve the walk along the Pilgrims' Way to Wrotham, but dismissed this idea, as my companions would have had to wait and we would not reach our destination for the day by evening. I even thought of returning after we had completed the pilgrimage and walking the missing miles. But it was too late to mend the situation; we had made a mistake and I had to live with it.

I was sure there was something to be learnt from this episode, but it was quite a few weeks before I realized its significance in relation to the inner life. I was talking to a theologian friend about the incident, still wondering why I had been so upset. 'Scrupulousness,' he said, adding that in terms of the spiritual life this could lead to the sins of obstinacy and despair. This rang true, so I checked the definition of the word. It comes from the Latin *scrupulus* meaning a small, sharp stone and scrupulosity 'may be the result of much ascetic reading of a rigorist tendency, *but more often is the outcome of nervous disturbances*.'[1] That seemed to settle the matter (I am all too aware of my 'nervous disturbances') until I thought of the opposite of scrupulosity, which is surely sloth. If I gave in to every opportunity to accept a lift, to take the easiest path, I could hardly be said to be making a pilgrimage at all. There seemed to be a strong argument in favour of the Middle Way.

I was glad that I had visited Kemsing on a previous occasion, because our wanderings on the North Downs Way had taken us well north of the village. The medieval pilgrims could not have seen the curving eighteenth century 'crinkle-crankle' wall along one side of the churchyard, or the modern window showing Thomas Becket in the company of Saint Richard of Chichester. But for a while Kemsing was a place of pilgrimage in its own right and they would not have passed without praying before the statue of Saint Edith and perhaps drinking from the well that still bears her name. She was the daughter of King Edward the Peaceful and was famed both for her piety and for her bounty to the local people, who used to bring their grain to be blessed at her shrine.

Once in Wrotham, after our circuitous deviation, we were back on the Pilgrims' Way, indeed the Bull Inn is a fourteenth-century coaching inn, once a stopping place for pilgrims. We wandered round the delightful old village, trying to imagine how the archbishop's palace must once have looked, then visited the church. Here, as at the churches of St James at Shere and Saint Martha's, there are a number of little crosses incised into a piece of sandstone, often thought to indicate the passing of pilgrims, though the writer of the pamphlet on sale at the church thinks that it is more likely that the crosses were to ward off evil spirits. Before we continued on our way we took advantage of being in a quiet village during working hours to do some shopping. Jane bought a bottle of wine for the evening and told us of the following exchange. 'Haven't seen you before. Where do you come from?' 'From Winchester' she said, 'and we're going to Canterbury.' 'OOH' he said, clearly impressed, 'Thomas Becket?' 'Yes, that's right. I'll say a prayer for you.' 'Lovely. Nobody's ever done that for me before.'

We left Wrotham, crossed the M20 and followed the Downs in a north-easterly sweep along another of those long stretches where the North Downs Way, the Pilgrims' Way and the Trackway are harmoniously one and the same. After the morning's confused clambering this was perfect walking, confidence about the way once more leaving space for thought and rhythmic continuity of movement. I was learning to be grateful for these moments rather than begrudging their rarity; to accept that walking cannot always, or even often, be a smooth continuous whole any more than can life and that the opposites weave an intricate pattern before reaching wholeness. Pilgrimage means dovetailing with other people's speeds and inclinations; if one walker is compelled to stop and talk to every passing dog and another has to stop to change a film at what is, for the others, quite the wrong moment, so be it. I should admit that I, with my constant note-taking and occasional bursts of speed, probably provided more grounds for irritation than anyone.

So on this stretch we found we were walking physically separately yet in amiable companionship. There were woods on the hills above us, exuberant arable fields to our right, chalk underfoot and, as always, cow parsley embroidering the verges. We passed Platt Hill Wood, Hognore Wood and a house appropriately named Pilgrim House, from where we could see Trottiscliffe Church, which by then we knew was pronounced 'Trosley'. Then along the south side of Great Wood until we reached the turning to the Coldrum Stones, which lie just half a mile off the Pilgrims' Way.

I had been longing for this moment; I had visited the Coldrum Stones before and found the site infinitely moving. It is a Neolithic long barrow, and in 1910 excavators found the bones of twenty-two people, men, women and children, some of which were taken to Trottiscliffe Church. The bones revealed that these people were short and strong in stature, with long heads and broad feet. The bones of ox, cat, deer, rabbit and fox suggest that they were meat eaters and their teeth were healthy, but the elderly apparently suffered from rheumatism and all the shin bones were flattened by the squatting posture they favoured. They were members of the Neolithic farming community who were the first to settle in this part of Kent and these twenty-two people were among the most prestigious of the community, possibly even members of a royal family.

Careful study of the barrow and the bones during the excavation suggested that the bodies of the dead were laid in a separate wooden structure until the flesh had rotted, then, when the bones fell apart, they were gathered up, separated and placed in the tombs with great care. Though the religious beliefs of Neolithic farming communities are not known, experts believe that the planning and thought given to these long barrows speak of well-organized communities with a belief in some sort of life after death. To anyone interested in the universal symbolism underlying different religions, it is interesting that the larger end of long barrows, containing the main sepulchre, frequently point, as do the altars of Christian churches, in an easterly direction. The distinguished archaeologist Jacquetta Hawkes goes further, suggesting that these monuments must have served as religious meeting places and that the cult associated with the tombs was concerned with ideas of rebirth.

> I do not think it is allowing the imagination too great liberty to say that the faith, for it is very truly a faith, which made the New Stone Age communities labour to drag, raise, pile thousands of tons of stone and earth, was in resurrection, the resurrection of their corn and beasts, of themselves. They laid their dead in the dark, earth-enclosed chamber with something of the same conviction with which they cast the seed corn into the soil. [2]

I have never understood why some Christians are threatened by pre-Christian religions, by the fact that there were crucified saviours before Christ, that the idea of the Trinity appeared in Egyptian and Indian religions long before Christianity and that, as Jacquetta Hawkes writes, the idea of resurrection goes back to the Stone Age and probably beyond. That Christianity draws on earlier religions, which themselves draw deep from the human psyche, seems to me to confirm the depth of its wisdom.

As we neared the site I wondered if this ancient place would strike me again with the force of my first visit. There they were, the massive stones, four standing upright in the centre, many more fallen to the ground in a peristalith, a stone circle. The light was bright, the wind blustering round as it had blustered for four thousand years; the grass mown close and clean, the simple fence surrounding the burial chamber discreet and solid. Knowing almost nothing about this family with my head, to my heart they seemed familiar and loveable. I was tempted to scramble over the fence to touch the stones, to get closer to those far-off ancestors; it was respect that prevented me. I felt the need to cross myself, restrained again by respect for the pagan bones, whose God may not have wanted that particular action. This was a pilgrimage in itself. This was holy ground.

Too moved for discussion, we stayed silently for some time. I was standing at the back of the circle of stones, looking east, when suddenly I saw, in the far distance and exactly above the central stone, the spire of Birling Church. It was a wonderful moment of completion; the burial chamber, built by pagans seeking resurrection in their way, the Christian church, proclaiming the resurrection of Christ.

It was fitting to our mood that, for the next two nights, we should be staying at The Friars, the Aylesford home of a community of Carmelites. It was founded in 1242, when the first Carmelites arrived from the Holy Land. Five years later Saint Simon Stock, who was believed to have been born in Kent (a late tradition even suggests Aylesford itself) was elected prior general of the order. During his time the tension between those who wished to remain hermits and those wanting to become friars was resolved and the Carmelites became an international order, with foundations in Oxford, Cambridge, Paris and Bologna.

There is a tradition that Saint Simon experienced a vision of the Mother of God, who touched his scapular and promised her protection to anyone who wore one. This gave rise to the 'Scapular devotion', popular with many Roman Catholics and though one of the brothers told me it is 'soft-pedalled' at The Friars, it is honoured with a carved plaque of the vision in one of the chapels and a medieval wooden statue, normally in the Relic Chapel but carried in procession during the pilgrimages. The Relic Chapel is so called because in it is a tall reliquary covered with ceramic tiles and housing the saint's skull, in 1951 it was brought back from Bordeaux, where he had died nearly seven hundred years before.

After the Dissolution of the Monasteries the house became a private dwelling and it was not until 1949 that it returned to the friars, Carmelites from all over the world contributing to the recovery of their ancient home. Almost immediately coach loads of people began coming to Aylesford to pray and The Friars became, by popular acclaim, a Marian shrine and a place of pilgrimage. A great deal of work – not to mention money – has been devoted to restoring the old buildings and now The Friars is not only the home of a small community, but a well-established conference and retreat centre with five chapels and a guesthouse accommodating up to a hundred people. Its main purpose is to be a centre for prayer and pilgrimage and the friars estimate around 200,000 people come every year, when the weather permits gathering in a huge outdoor area known as the Piazza or Shrine Area.

The old buildings, lovingly renovated, were glowing in golden evening light when we arrived. We collected our keys from the reception desk and settled into our rooms on one side of the huge old courtyard. We were delighted to find them not only spacious, but with timbered walls and ceilings, some of the beams dating from the twelfth century, some added in the same style during the twentieth-century reconstruction and so well done it was hard to tell the difference. We were delighted, too, to find that there were hot pipes running round the rooms, enabling us to wash and dry our clothes. We opened Jane's bottle of wine and spent an hour chatting and admiring the pictures Barbara had been painting while we walked, before going over to the Pilgrims' Hall for our evening meal.

In this beautiful hall I was aware, with a particular poignancy, of the pilgrims who had been before us. They would have known these stone walls, these satisfying proportions; they would have sat at wooden tables very like the one at which we were sitting. They would even have looked up at the same oak beams in the roof, for when the hall was restored the original beams were in such good condition that they did not need to be replaced, they were simply cleaned off and put back where they had been for hundreds of years. In fact when they were sent for carbon dating they were found to date from 1170, the very year of Becket's martyrdom. So the assumption must be that the hall was built in time for the first pilgrims who travelled to the saint's shrine at Canterbury.

After a good helping of cauliflower cheese I explored the two galleries above the dining hall. One is now a library and the small top gallery is at the moment unused, but for the early pilgrims they were the sleeping quarters. There would have been a big log fire in the middle of the hall and a hole in the roof allowing the smoke to escape. Above this hole there would probably have been a square wooden structure to keep out the rain, or at least the worst of it. The softwood balustrades round the galleries are now open railings, though they would originally have been panelled to keep the draughts from the sleeping pilgrims.

The day ended with night prayer - it is sad that so many religious houses are dropping the old names for the Office, and it is no longer known as Compline - in the small Cloister Chapel. It was very quiet and straightforward; in fact it was its very ordinariness that impressed me. This was how the friars ended their day, every day. While we were with them, this was how we would end ours.

PADDLESWORTH CHAPEL

Chapter Fourteen

The Coldrum Stones to Broad Street

Jewels in Shadowland

For the last three or four days the pilgrimage had become my world. There was a sense in which time had begun ten days before, anything earlier was a faint memory, the future beyond imagining. So too did space, my physical world, begin at Winchester and end at Canterbury. I was living in the here and now with an intensity I had seldom previously experienced. Occupying this tiny point in time and space it was, like the mystical point, infinite. Whatever the minor irritations and frustrations, despite upsurges of violent emotion and pain, I was, at a deep level, content.

Perhaps pilgrimage was purging my guilt, for I no longer felt uneasy as we drove back on our tracks from Aylesford to the place where we had stopped the night before; the two miles from the Coldrum Stones to Paddlesworth Church were also in keeping with my peaceful mood. The track continued its gentle sweep round the foot of the Downs, the day was slightly misty and sultry, but quiet and warm. Perhaps most important of all we were still near enough to the Stones to feel under their timeless sway. There was a long stretch when we walked through trees, enclosed in a tunnel of branches meeting over our heads with a womb-like protectiveness. We walked mostly in silence, something we had intended to do more often had it not been for the demands of maps and signposts, not to mention our own loquacity.

In Belloc's time the little chapel at Paddlesworth was a ruin and twenty years ago Sean Jennet found it had been 'long since desecrated and is now a barn attached to a linhay'. We are indebted to the Redundant Churches Fund, an independent charity who took it over in 1976, for its restoration. It is a tiny, squat, yet beautifully proportioned Norman building, standing alone and vulnerable on the edge of a field, opposite a farm. It would have been known to the medieval pilgrims and can just lay claim to be a living church once more, for it is open at weekends and services are held there twice a year.

The village of Snodland (it can blame a Saxon landowner called Snodd for its unattractive name) spills over almost into Paddlesworth and on its outskirts stands Woodlands Farm, a half-timbered house with a long and eventful history. I had heard about it in the bar of The Bull Inn at Wrotham. 'You must go and see my parents,' said the girl from whom I had just bought a drink. 'They live in a house that used to be a pilgrim hospice.'

Mr and Mrs Meyers greeted me warmly and showed me round the house. It was built in 1450, but the foundations could have been much earlier. Neolithic axes found nearby indicate the presence of prehistoric peoples and there are signs that there was once a Saxon barn on the site. Its use by pilgrims was indicated by an outside staircase, no longer there, which led to an upstairs room. Apparently the pilgrims would have gone straight up to sleep, without disturbing the owners, who trusted them to settle up in the morning before they went on their way.

The Meyers also told me something of the local history surrounding the Pilgrims' Way in that part of Kent. For instance how William Caxton married a girl from the nearby village of Halling and set up a printing press there; of a seventeenth-century owner of Woodlands Farm who started the first scheme for apprentices, which still helps the young people of Snodland. In more macabre vein, I heard about how people thought to be witches were tried in the ecclesiastical court in Snodland and how those found guilty were condemned to death by drowning. The Medway at this point is a deep and dangerous river and the women were put in a damaged old boat, the oldest pushed to the front where they would perish soonest. A point of the river was chosen where the tide was fast and the boat was then pushed mercilessly out into the turbulent waters.

It would be nice if the third story were true. There is a legend that says that Jesus travelled here with Joseph of Arimathea. It is said that he came up the river, passed the front door of the Roman villa whose remains have been found near its banks, and walked part of the Pilgrims' Way.

There was once a ferry across the Medway at Snodland, used by Belloc, who claims also to have seen a hard-bottomed ford. It would then have been only a short walk, passing Burham and Little Culand, to the megalithic monument known as Kit's Coty House. Now there is neither ferry nor ford and plans for a bridge have not yet materialized, so the nearest points to cross the river are to the north, over the Medway bridge near Rochester, or to the south, at Aylesford. The North Downs Way leaves the Pilgrims' Way just before Paddlesworth and makes a huge loop to Rochester and down again to Kit's Coty. The Aylesford route takes a shorter detour to the south, meeting the other two routes at the White Horse Stone near Kit's Coty.

Over a cup of coffee we discussed the options and considered ways in which we could reach Burham, tantalizingly close across the river. We had been told that it was sometimes possible to hire a boat, but we should have made arrangements beforehand, as none of the locals seemed very sure who to approach. We resisted a passing ~ and quite unrealistic ~ tempation to follow Belloc's example and 'borrow' a boat, in the end opting for the shortest route, which would take us right past The Friars, where we were staying.

We had made a pragmatic and unwise choice; it was a dreadful walk. I would sooner have trebled the distance than walk those few miles. I wondered how Cobbett would have fumed over the monstrosities bequeathed to us by the twentieth century, for not only were we deprived of the river crossing, but saw our industrial heritage revealed in its worst and drabbest colours as we made our way down the river's side. Now I knew why someone has called the Medway 'the dustbin of Kent'.

We started through a maze of modern buildings, across a car park and under a railway bridge. The Blue Circle Lake had sounded attractive, and it was at least a redeeming feature, but soon we were funnelled between wire fences close to the railway line, processed through a trading estate and across the track by New Hythe Station. Then, squeezed between more wire fences, now even higher and stretched over concrete posts, we came into a bleak industrial area that at the time I thought was Reeds Paper Mills. Our senses, spoilt by so much countryside, were assaulted on all sides; downland now replaced by charmless factories, hedgerows by these forbidding fences, the fresh wind by a heavy sulphurous smell. I discovered later that the paper mills had been bought up by a Swedish packaging business and that the most likely explanation for the smell was the coal-fired boiler house that produces steam for drying the paper. Apparently burning coal in bulk can produce an acrid smell.

Once through the factory buildings we were walking on the towpath and assumed that the worst was over. But before we had time to breathe a sigh of relief I saw that not only was the Medway at this point sluggish and dirty, but that one vile smell was giving way to another, even worse. The reason was not far to seek. As we rounded a bend in the river, there was the sign - SEWER. We were now passing the local sewerage works.

My reaction to these scenes of desolation surprised me - I was glad, just as I had been glad that the previous Sunday had given us a taste of walking in really dreadful weather. Apart from frequent confrontations with motorways and traffic, we had spent most of the last ten days in quiet, sometimes idyllic, countryside. If pilgrimage is an image of life then it too must have its shadow side. In meeting ugliness, harsh restrictions, smells, even the ultimate symbol of the dark side of life, excrement and dirt, the totality of life was more accurately reflected. This was brought poignantly home as across the river, nestling in this tulgy industrial wasteland, we saw the sparkling old houses of the village of Aylesford. Jewels can exist in shadowland.

We had lunch in one of Aylesford's oldest pubs, only half a mile from The Friars, and continued along our enforced detour, modernity still oppressing us as we passed Safeway's massive storage depot. Once we had left that eyesore behind, the route took us past a cherry orchard and into fields, but the depression of the morning still hung over me, most palpably in the constant throb of traffic from the M20. On these occasions I was quite grateful for my continuing (though slightly improving) deafness and wondered, as I had wondered many times before, whether there was a reason for this unexpected loss of hearing. It was certainly a protection against the noise of traffic, but by making conversation difficult, could it also be forcing my attention inwards? Just as the writer of Ecclesiastes claimed that 'to everything there is a season and a time to every purpose under the heaven', so too nothing is without a reason – the problem is to find what that reason is.

My spirits rose at the thought of the three prehistoric monuments we were approaching – the Countless Stones, Kit's Coty House and the White Horse Stone. We saw first the Countless Stones, which from a distance appeared to Jacquetta Hawkes as 'a small shoal of stranded whales'.[1] We must have seen them from even farther away, for they could have been mistaken for sleeping sheep. They have fallen in such a way that it is not always easy to tell where one stone ends and another begins, and some say that they are called 'countless' simply because there are so many and because they lie so confusingly; others that a magic spell cast over them prevents them from ever being correctly counted. The only certainty is that they once formed a burial chamber, a thought that became very real when I learnt that the holes in the hillside may once have been the rudimentary homes of the folk who worshipped there.

Kit's Coty House is a megalithic tomb, one of the best known prehistoric monuments in the whole country. It stands in a cornfield called Bluebell Hill just over a mile northeast of Aylesford, three massive upright stones supporting a fourth. It too was almost certainly a burial chamber and an eighteenth-century drawing shows that there was a long barrow running westward from it. Even in the seventeenth century it was sufficiently well known for the diarist Samuel Pepys to break his journey and visit it. He wrote that the stones were 'of great bigness, although not so big as those on Salisbury Plain. But certainly a thing of great antiquity, and I am mightily glad to see it'.[2]

So was I, but I have to admit to being disappointed. The imagination is stirred by the theory that it marked the burial place of Catigern, a British chief killed nearby in the battle against the Jutes, Hengist and Horsa; even more by the thought that it was probably known to cave-dwellers who worshipped the sun. A more down-to-earth version suggests that a humble shepherd known simply as Christopher sheltered from the winds under the great stones. But I had no sense of a living link with ancestors, of the place still being inhabited by the spirits of the dead, as I had at the Coldrum Stones.

The last of these old stones was the White Horse Stone, a large sarsen stone, standing unceremoniously by the side of the lane, now once again the Pilgrims' Way. We walked round, peering at it from many different angles, until at last, like seeing a face in the clouds, we could trace the form of a horse's head, its eye a deep hole in the stone. We then realized there were the remains of a fire beside it and wondered if modern Druids or witches had been sacrificing before it. If they had

I hoped that they did so in a spirit of respect.

After another mile the sign to Boxley forced me to leave prehistoric times and to leap some four thousand years to the Middle Ages, by contrast now seeming quite close to the twentieth century. It has been suggested that Boxley received special attention at the Dissolution of the Monasteries, as it was here that the adjudicator sat and here that he decided against Henry's divorce; certainly there is little left of the twelfth-century Cistercian abbey, now a private house and far too close to the M20 for the comfort of the owners. However, Boxley Abbey is still remembered for the two miraculous images that were shown to pilgrims, the image of the child Saint Rumbold and the celebrated crucifix, the Rood of Grace.

Tradition has it that the miraculous crucifix arrived at the monastery on the back of a stray packhorse, which refused to leave until the monks had given the sacred object a home. It turned out to have extraordinary powers, the hands sometimes raised in blessing, the head able to bow in sorrow and the face assuming different expressions as the eyes rolled or wept and the mouth moved. These gifts were not put to pious use, for whether the image expressed pleasure (by its heavenly smile) or sadness (by a disappointed frown) was dependent not on the state of the pilgrim's soul, but on the size of his offering.

But worse was to come. After the Dissolution the man employed to pull down the buildings made a disconcerting discovery. He wrote to Thomas Cromwell that he had found in the Rood of Grace

> Certain engines and old wire, with rotten old sticks in the back, which caused the eyes to move and stir in the head thereof, like unto a living thing, and also the nether lip likewise to move as though it should speak, which was not a little strange to him and to others present.[3]

The iconoclasts loved this, though some bishops had been aware of the fraud and had chosen to look the other way, even to defend these fraudulent images. I cannot help hoping that naïve pilgrims, cheered by a 'heavenly smile', did not discover that they had been cheated.

The image of Saint Rumbold also involved deception. He must have been quite the youngest saint, for he died at three days old, having already recited the Lord's Prayer and the Apostles' Creed - hence his canonization. This small statue had the power to change its weight at will. Sometimes it could be moved by a child, on other occasions it resisted the greatest strength, it all depended (or so it was believed) on the state of the soul of the pilgrim. Women who had lost their chastity stood to risk public exposure, for to them Saint Rumbold would be as immovable as the walls of the abbey itself. An offering to the priest could spare their blushes - he would operate some hidden device behind a nearby pillar and the statue moved freely.

Neither of these images can be seen today, and as we stood at this turning to Boxley we were propelled into the twentieth century by roadworks, for at this point their presence had diverted all the local traffic onto the Pilgrims' Way. The lane was so narrow that a small van brushed the cow parsley on both sides at once, there were no verges and it was - as it always seemed to be when we reached these narrow lanes - rush hour. This time I had no qualms (perhaps I was learning to cope with scruples) and flagged down the first car going in our direction. It was a large white Mercedes driven by a charming Indian businessman, so we travelled the remaining mile into Detling in the utmost comfort. I recalled 'the chariot in weariness' we prayed for when Canon Teare read the *Itinerarium* and wondered if 'a protection in danger' might not fit the case rather better. But this time my conscience was clear - or do I protest too much?

We were tired by then, but after a drink at The Cock Horse (so named as it kept a horse to hitch to coaches and help them up hills) I felt refreshed, so I left my companions in the pub and carried on a little farther. This was partly inclination, partly that as we had made a small mistake in our calculations we realized that we would not reach Canterbury by midday on Saturday unless we did a little extra. The two and a half miles to Broad Street was another of those ecstatic walks, the Downs rising gently to my left and the fields bathed in a rosy evening light. I was quite sorry when I saw the car and my three companions coming to pick me up.

The evening was a high point in the pilgrimage, for not only were we royally entertained by Tikki and Blair Gulland but the occasion was given a particular poignancy because they were unknown to us, the only link being that Tikki's mother was a friend of Barbara's. This generosity to virtual strangers - dirty and tired strangers at that - made me think of the hospitality of the desert, of the days when hospitality was a sacred duty, of the instinctive kindness of man to man now so often drowned out by the pressure of modern life, perhaps even more by fear.

Apart from the pleasure of the Gullands' hospitality, receiving this warm welcome somehow gave us status as pilgrims. The medieval pilgrim would have been entertained without cost, indeed charity to pilgrims was assumed - in the eighth century a pilgrim was entitled to 'a roof over his head, a fire, wholesome water, and fresh bread'.[4] No pilgrim seeking monastic hospitality would be refused; they would be met by a senior monk, the kiss of peace exchanged and food, drink and a place to sleep offered. In fact the monasteries of the early Eastern Church were *required* to receive pilgrims and the tradition was incorporated into the Western Church, notably by the Benedictines, who laid aside money for hospitality to pilgrims; indeed one of whose abbots was renowned for personally washing the feet of every pilgrim. When, on busy pilgrimage routes, there were too many pilgrims for the monasteries to accommodate, guest halls and independent hospices run by the monks were specially built. The *Guide for*

Pilgrims to Santiago shows that this is not only good Christian practice but enlightened self-interest, for 'Whoever receives them receives Saint James and God himself.'

Admittedly the practice did not always live up to the theory, for the monasteries did not provide great comfort. Jonathan Sumption says that life for the pilgrims was 'monotonous and comfortless . . . in many hospices no food was served at all . . . Where there were beds, they were usually dirty, and fleas were a common incident of life in a hospice.'[5] Mostly the pilgrims slept on straw-covered floors and rats and mice were frequent visitors.

The more prosperous pilgrims could, and often did, find greater comfort in inns and taverns, but they were far from luxurious; no one would expect a bed to himself, meals were expensive and servants dishonest. But then, as now, standards varied. Chaucer's pilgrims were given a great welcome at 'that high-class hostelry known as The Tabard', where

> Everyone
> Was given a place and supper was begun.
> He served the finest victuals you could think,
> The wine was strong and we were glad to drink.[6]

Sumptuous banquets were given to visiting royalty and prelates, but the ordinary pilgrim had to be content with humbler fare. Or worse. A contemporary chronicler writing of medieval innkeepers records that

> There was no crime that they did not commit. They displayed fine wines and served cheap ones. Their fish was bad and their meat putrid. Their candles I did not burn. Their beds were filthy. They gave change in bad coin. Their inns were often brothels and always dens of drunkenness.[7]

But at least they were cheap – a bed cost less than a penny a head.

In receiving the hospitality of the Gullands we had the benefit of both their warm welcome and the comfort of their beautiful home. We drank a great deal of good wine, ate a delicious fish pie and talked until our exhaustion took over and we returned for a second night of monastic hospitality at The Friars.

'A GOOD TAVERN INN'

Chapter Fifteen

Broad Street to Westwell

In praise of pubs

B efore we continue on our way to Canterbury, let me take you on a short detour to visit Leeds Castle. It is not on the Old Road and I had no reason to believe it was visited by early pilgrims. My wish to visit it was peripheral to this particular route, but very relevant to the nature of pilgrimage in general - I could not resist the chance to walk another maze. Having walked the unicursal maze on St Catherine's Hill and seen how that was a microcosm of pilgrimage, I wanted to have the experience of walking a multicursal maze. As it was at least two miles off the route - and meant crossing the M20 at that - I had visited it some weeks before.

All the world was there, enjoying the first spring flowers, admiring the famous moated castle, an island fortress whose stones span a thousand years, from the ninth century, when it was the site of a manor of the Saxon royal family, to the elegant drawing room created in the 1930s. We milled around, eating ice creams, drank cups of undrinkable tea, then wandered round the lake. I could hardly take in the beautiful gardens, so impatient was I to reach the maze. It was planted in 1987 with 2,400 yew trees and knowing I would be faced with choice I was apprehensive. 'Children love getting lost in the maze and it's fun for grown-ups too' says the leaflet cheerily, but I, born under Pisces, the two fish swimming in opposite directions, was not so sure. I have more than my share of Piscean indecisiveness.

My premonitions were right. Seconds after I set foot between the trees, still only some three or four feet high, the first choice was presented to me. Did I turn left? Or right? Or go straight on? There was no reason to choose one or the other and I was filled with panic. The panic increased as choice followed choice among the small winding paths between the young trees. Eventually a certain nonchalance took over and I began to take one or the other path in an arbitrary way that contained little emotion; in no time I was within a stone's throw of the centre. What had I been worrying about? It was quite easy after all. Fool's gold ~ I was not there at all, the centre smiled triumphantly at me, unattainable beyond a line of trees I had thought I could penetrate but could not.

What should I do? Perhaps the gallant thing would be to cast myself into the darkness and head for the outside, to risk all and thus to succeed. Feeling brave and confident, rather like leaning outwards on a ski-slope, I took the path that seemed to lead away from the centre. It was, as I half suspected, too self-conscious a move and once again I was choosing one path after the other and going nowhere. The initial feeling of slightly drunken panic was changing into irritation and downright anger. How silly it all was, this endless trudging, these interminable paths and futile choices. And why did the centre hold such magnetic attraction for me? I needed to reach the centre so much that were it to be the home of death himself, still I had to get there. If I found myself flung right out of the maze by some wrong choice ~ THAT would be failure. The centre was where I had to be, whatever monster lurked there. So, interminably, now in a daze of confusion, a maze of delusion, I walked, no longer caring much which path I took. 'Nearly there!' said a voice somewhere on my right. And I was.

No sense of achievement. No reason for any turn, any choice. My only conscious decision, to cast away from the centre, had been wrong. Once there I had no wish to stay, it held no magic. I was not sorry when it was time to close and the keeper told us that the easiest way out was through the grotto. Panic again. Which was worse, to retrace my blind steps and risk getting lost as I sought escape, or to go underground, into the dark depths ninety feet beneath the maze. I chose the grotto, impressed at the imagination of its creators as I entered the still dark womb of the unconscious resting quietly under the tortuous winding paths of life. Then, at last, the return to light and air and the spacious park.

I was 'amazed' (yes, the words are philologically connected) at the difference between walking a unicursal and a multicursal maze. The unicursal gave me a sense of trust – I knew that I had just to keep going and I would reach the centre. On the other hand the multicursal, infuriating though it was with its bewildering and apparently pointless choices, seemed a more accurate mirror of life, so I was surprised to discover that for the first three thousand years of its history, until the Middle Ages, the maze was unicursal. Perhaps art was reflecting life. When life was simpler it was just a question of survival, of keeping going along one's given path; as life became more complex, as choices multiplied, so did the maze become multicursal. Pilgrimage, I now knew from experience, included both. There were those delightful occasions when there was no doubt as to the route and walking was, if not easy, at least uncomplicated; and there were the moments of confusion, doubt and choice. So too the spiritual pilgrimage includes both, though I suspect most people find – I certainly do – that they spend more time on ways of confusion than on ways of simplicity.

But to continue on our rightful route. We had stopped at Broad Street the night before, so it was to Broad Street we returned that morning, the eleventh day of our pilgrimage. This was to be a day when the path was clear and uninterrupted – a unicursal day – and though that did not stop us twice taking a wrong turn we were soon at Hollingbourne. As we had been dismayed by what the twentieth century had done to the stretch between Snodland and Aylesford, so we were shamed by our first glimpse of Hollingbourne. One of its pubs, directly on the Pilgrims' Way, used to be called the Pilgrims' Rest, it was later known as the King's Head. It has now been given a name which reflects the seamier side of our contemporary life and is not even a good joke – the beautiful old house displays a sign reading 'The Dirty Habit'.

Hollingbourne, once home of the Culpeper family, is a beautiful village, none the less. A red brick Elizabethan manor house crowns a street of houses so perfect that Richard Church, writing in 1948, was lulled into fantasies of a life already becoming history when he wrote:

> I cannot think of a more suitable village than Hollingbourne in which to spend one's latter years. To settle there, in one of its period houses (I should choose a William and Mary piece higher up the village), with a devoted gardener, a good cellar of claret, and rooms in the Albany so that comfortable reading should be done in London when in the mood, seems to me the height of civilized living. [1]

We were tempted to linger in Hollingbourne, but it was too early in the day for leisurely stops, the day was fine and the countryside beckoned. For the rest of the morning, from Hollingbourne to Lenham, the Way was so straight that it could have been a Roman road and as the path took us over rough dirt tracks and soft grassy paths, over gravel, chalk, hard flinty clay and occasionally a metalled surface I became very aware of the importance of what lay underfoot; the texture of the ground became another tactile element in the sensual pleasure of walking. For some miles we walked along the edges of arable fields, the Downs rising on our left, providing a constant reassurance and sense of direction. I felt deeply content, even glad when at one point we took a wrong turn, for we found ourselves under a beech avenue arching so gracefully over our heads that we welcomed the mistake.

The day was marred only by rape – I mean oil seed rape. All

around us, for mile after mile, stretched endless acres of that glaring, shallow yellow that has become such a faceless feature of spring in northern Europe. No doubt it brings millions of pounds to the farmers, but it adds nothing to the countryside and is harmful to brassicas and humans alike. Local gossip has it that one of these farmers has not only reduced much of Kent to prairie land, but has also twice been in prison for cutting down trees illegally. Curiously they had to admit he was a good farmer, a conclusion that did not seem to follow very logically.

A short diversion across a field brought us to Lenham in time for lunch. This is another delightful village, boasting a magnificent tithe barn, a sixteenth-century Forge House and the 'Saxon Warrior's Chemist', so named as a Saxon grave was discovered under the half-timbered house. In the heart of the square is an seventeenth-century pub called The Dog and Bear and there we settled down to wait for Barbara.

I would like to sing a paean of praise for the pubs along the Pilgrims' Way. The pub became for us a symbol of comfort, hospitality and welcome. We would arrive hot and tired, strew our rucksacks and jackets along benches, shed our shoes under the table, drink shandies and relax as if in our own sitting rooms. Sometimes, for the price of a drink and a sandwich, perhaps later a cup of coffee, we would spend over an hour talking, resting, using the telephone, seeking advice from whoever was at the bar. Nobody bothered us, hurried us on or even seemed to notice us particularly - we were simply allowed to BE. Pubs were our second homes and publicans the salt of the earth. 'There is nothing which has yet been contrived by man,' wrote Samuel Johnson, 'by which so much happiness is produced as by a good tavern or inn.' I had to agree with him.

We were not in a hurry to leave the comfort of The Dog and Bear, but eventually we made our way back to the Pilgrims' Way across a field, slightly alarmed by popping sounds, as if we were being shot at (it was, we learnt later, a device intended to scare the birds, not us) and rejoining the North Downs Way on a greensward path by a huge chalk war memorial. We were well on schedule to complete the day's walk and that reassurance, coupled with the charm of the day and the hospitality of The Dog and Bear, had left us very relaxed, so when the glare of the remorseless rape gave way to soft green cornfields and sheep, we celebrated by lying down and having a dram – well diluted with water – from the hip flask I had been given for the pilgrimage. This was the life – lying by a cornfield, chatting.

Then we dropped off the route again to visit Charing, where the archbishops had a manor house which Becket would undoubtedly have visited as he went about his diocesan business and where Henry VIII is believed to have stayed. The remains of the palace are now a farm and can only just be glimpsed beyond a notice saying 'Private', but the main street, with its Georgian house frontages, is so charming that I could not see how the village could have earned its unkind slogan:

Dirty Charing lies in a hole
Has but one bell and that she stole.

It was the church, built on a site given by King Ethelbert of Kent, that most interested me, for in the Middle Ages the pilgrims would have visited it to see Charing's famous relic – the block on which the head of John the Baptist was struck off. It was believed to have been brought from the Holy Land by Richard Cœur de Lion, but even if it escaped the attention of King Henry VIII's commissioners it would certainly have been destroyed in 1590, when a fire, started by a Spaniard shooting into the dry shingles of the roof, caused serious damage to the church. I had little heart for so gruesome a trophy, but the cult of relics was at the heart of pilgrimage, so, walking as I was in medieval footsteps, I was curious to understand something of their power, to know how they would have been a source of forgiveness, guidance and healing. But to do so I would have to bury my prejudices.

Orthodox and Roman Catholic Christians believe that 'the grace of God present in the saints' bodies during life remains active in their relics when they have died, and that God uses these relics as a channel of divine power and an instrument of healing'.[2] This sophisticated theology of the body puts the whole subject onto a level that I would like to understand, but have to admit to finding difficult. More accessible is the idea that in essence the veneration of relics is based on the natural instinct to revere objects associated with the beloved dead. I am hardly in a position to criticize that. My house is filled with things I treasure because they were my husband's. I keep old clothes I no longer wear simply because he gave them to me, house boxes of useless junk that he had never got round to throwing away, treasure a broken statue we once bought together. I know that it is absurd, that hanging on to possessions will not bring him back, but in my weakness I need them. One day I may be able to free myself from them – and perhaps that is the point. It is not that there is anything wrong with loving objects connected with the dead, but in *needing* them, in being attached to them, in attributing too much to them.

The earliest evidence of the worship of relics by Christians was in the second century when the bones of the martyred Bishop Polycarp were considered 'more valuable than precious stones and finer than refined gold' and the cult spread so quickly that soon the Church was forced to react. It was divided on the issue, both criticizing and defending. In response to fierce denunciations of relics made by Vigilantius, a priest writing at the turn of the fourth century, St Jerome offered the classic Christian justification:

We do not worship their relics any more than we do the sun or the moon, the angels, archangels, or seraphims. We honour them in honour of He whose faith they witnessed. We honour the Master by means of the servants.[3]

In practice, however, the honour shown to the remains of the servants often rivalled the honour given to the Master; relics were not only worshipped with undiscriminating devotion but healing properties were attributed to them. Often very important relics were so carefully housed and guarded that they could not be seen, certainly they could not be touched, so pilgrims would seek healing from the humblest objects that had been in contact with the saint's body - dust, stones, scraps of paper. The examples are legion. For instance after the body of St Cuthbert was found to be incorrupt a demoniac boy was believed to have been cured by drinking soil, moist from the water that had washed the body.[4] St Gregory of Tours was cured of an eye infection by drinking wine that had been poured into the footstep of St Benigne.[5] Becket's followers claimed cures from 'the water of Thomas', but as the demand so greatly exceeded the supply, the dilution became weaker and weaker until the cure was effected by a liquid innocent of the slightest trace of the saint's blood. Examples of miraculous healings are so numerous that even sceptics must wonder if there is not something in it, if only that believing a cure is possible itself leads to cure.

The thriving market for relics led to false claims and embarrassing situations, for instance two churches asserting they possessed the same saint's head (a fate which also befell Haydn, Swedenborg and Schiller) and so many pieces of the True Cross being claimed as genuine that there would have been enough to make several complete crosses. Some claims were so bizarre, so ludicrous, that it is almost as if there was a move to make mock of the cult - for instance there were thought to be phials containing Mary's milk, Christ's tears, the tip of Lucifer's tail and the sound of the bells of Solomon's temple. Then there were those who claimed to possess the mark of Cain and some clay from the field in which God created Adam.

It is hard to see how those who dismembered the bodies of the saints could claim to be acting with honour or in love, but this happened with distressing regularity, most notably to St

Teresa of Avila, whose body has found its way all over the world. Most of her remains, including her heart and her right arm, are in Alba where she died, Rome boasts her right foot and a piece of her jaw, Lisbon has her left hand, Paris and Brussels a finger each and Mexico and Madrid have a portion of her flesh. Yet sometimes it was those who loved her most who dismembered her body. It was after all her great friend Jerónimo Gracián who cut off her little finger and wore it round his neck for the rest of his life.

The argument for the psychological element in miraculous cures is supported by the belief that faith in the relic was considered more important than whether it was guaranteed to be genuine; also by an Alice in Wonderland sort of argument which saw a cure as proof of a relic's authenticity. The Church, helpless in the face of popular devotion, could only counsel moderation, urging that no relic should be venerated without official authentication. Even this was honoured more in the breach than in the observance and, whether genuine or not, precious relics in magnificent reliquaries drew pilgrims in their thousands. There was also the seductive spin-off of the pilgrims' offerings, filling the coffers of the churches and monasteries that owned the relics.

In the eighth century official approval of the cult was implied when the Council of Nicaea forbade, under pain of excommunication, the consecration of any church without a relic and I was surprised to discover that as recently as 1977 the Vatican, advising on the rite of the dedication of a church and altar, declared that wherever possible there should be a relic under the altar. The change is only in emphasis – the words 'wherever possible' – though it is now explicit that it is better to have no relic than one of doubtful authenticity. So too do relics still stir the imagination. At a recent performance of Eliot's *Murder in the Cathedral* in Northamptonshire, one of the front seats was occupied by a bone of St Thomas. It normally lives in the church safe, but makes occasional special appearances.

Compared to Lenham, Charing gave us a poor welcome; it was a weekday afternoon in May, yet nothing was open – tearooms, pub and restaurant presenting us with firmly locked doors. Once we had seen the church we were not tempted to linger, but we had made good time and it was too early to return to Lenham, where we had arranged to meet, so we decided to go on to the village of Westwell. Though it was a pleasant evening walk, we had been over-optimistic. A wrong turning added a mile or two to our journey and by the time we reached Westwell we had walked nearly seventeen miles since morning and were utterly exhausted.

For me this was the high point of physical exhaustion so far; I had reached my limit and found some consolation in having this experience, but it was the last straw when we could not find a public telephone and the pub was as firmly closed as the Charing tea-rooms. We were just thinking we would have to knock on a friendly-looking door and hope to have the same luck we had at West Kingswood, when the pub opened and we were able to ring for a taxi to take us back to our meeting place in Lenham. It was like a home from home, to be able to spread ourselves gratefully over the hospitable benches of The Dog and Bear.

THE LAKE BY ST MARY'S CHURCH, EASTWELL

Chapter Sixteen

Westwell to Chilham

Time suspended

I t was Friday, 14 May, the twelfth day of our pilgrimage; we were less than twenty miles from the spot where Saint Thomas Becket was martyred, our journey's end and a place for hundreds of years regarded as holy ground. I did not realize that within a few miles we would be standing on ground that was not, as far as I know, made famous by visions or martyrdom, but which, to me at least, was a place of overwhelming holiness.

We set off from Westwell along one of those stretches so quiet and beautiful that my spirits were simultaneously lulled and raised; I was filled with that mysterious mixture of elation and peace that natural beauty can inspire. The young corn, barely a foot high, and as yet untouched by wind or weather, was soft as a baby's breath; it contrasted dramatically with a tough old oak across the field, victim to the great storm of 1989, lying in dignity despite being, against its nature, horizontal, with earth-seeking roots exposed.

St Mary's Church, Eastwell, is not on the Pilgrims' Way, but on this occasion I felt nothing but gratitude to the owners of Eastwell Park, whose notice 'Private Grounds. Keep Out' forces walkers onto a parallel path and thus past the church. It is a ruin now, its fine old bones shattered by the guns that were sited nearby during the Second World War; in 1951 it was again assaulted, this time by an unusually tempestuous wind. Now only the tower remains, a few walls and the vestige of once graceful windows.

The ruins stand alone, no other buildings are visible. There are trees close to the tower, some overshadowing it, others clustering round protectively. Rough grass borders a large, still lake to the south. I had rarely experienced so deep a sense of peace. I read the notice on the church tower: 'This ancient house of God is being repaired by the Friends of Friendless Churches . . . It remains a consecrated building and the churchyard is sacred ground. Please respect them accordingly.'

I was touched by this appeal, reminded yet again of that question at the heart of pilgrimage ~ what is sacred ground, what makes a holy place? Several weeks later I was reflecting on this question, when I had an appointment with a very remarkable cranial osteopath. After the treatment he told me to lie down quietly for an hour or so to let my back rest. I said that I would, adding, for no particular reason, that I would be thinking about sacred ground. 'Then think about the sacred place in yourself,' he said.

I was intrigued by this suggestion and lay thinking . . . it came with a flash of certainty, the certainty of experience which cannot be denied ~ the sacred place in myself was that place which could feel love. This realization put the whole idea into a different perspective. When pilgrims travel to sacred shrines, is it love they are seeking? If God is love and if sacred ground is a place where God is more present then yes, of course it is. I was blinded by my own stupidity. It was easy enough to connect the pilgrimage and the sacred place with God, but how could I have failed to connect the two inseparables God and love? So love that gives its life in sacrifice leaves its legacy of sanctity.

The awareness of a holy place is elusive, unavailable to us when we most long for it, striking us with the force of revelation when we least expect it. I have never forgotten my first visit to the Holy Land and my conviction of the presence of Jesus on the Sea of Galilee and in the quiet of the Judean hills. Then the shock of going to the Holy Sepulchre in Jerusalem and seeing priests from various denominations each lifting a cloth covering the tomb, saying, 'This is our piece.' 'Look, this is ours.' For me holiness fled from the place at that instant.

Yet I know that holy places can and do survive such treatment, that it is possible to see beyond the greed and possessiveness that can tarnish holy places. Holiness cannot easily be banished. T. S. Eliot writes, at the end of *Murder in the Cathedral*, that

> Wherever a saint has dwelt, wherever a martyr has
> given his blood for Christ,
> There is holy ground, and the sanctity shall not
> depart from it
> Though armies trample over it, though sightseers
> come with guidebooks looking over it.[1]

The sanctity may not have departed, but it can become harder to perceive.

Many places become sacred. We tend to think of Jerusalem, Mecca, Delphi or Stonehenge, but a sacred place can be much humbler, more personal. It might be a particular church, a rock or tree, a stretch of coastline. I have a friend who has made a little prayer place underneath the stairs – that is her sacred place. And Zen practitioners bow to the cushions on which they sit in *zazen*; it is a sacred place and must be honoured and kept special.

Whether a place is made sacred by its relationship to cosmological forces, like its position on a ley line, or whether because of the presence of a holy person, an apparition or a miraculous happening, the common thread seems to be the love that inspires mankind to pray and the power of prayer, ascending from that spot for many years. Years ago, staying in a large house in the Isle of Wight, I noticed that one small room, just off the sitting room, had a very special atmosphere, it felt charged with some power I could not identify. I stepped to and fro between the two rooms and it was like finding a warm place in the sea when you are bathing. They were different, there was no doubt about it. When I remarked on this to my host he told me that the house had once been owned by a religious order and that this was the room they used for private prayer.

For the writer Margaret Pawley the Abbey of Bec, in France, is a holy place, 'Because people have prayed there since the eleventh century. Three Archbishops of Canterbury, Lanfranc, Anselm and Theobald came from Bec and they have left something of themselves behind and you can get caught up in the life of it. Ordinary things being turned into sacred things. The difference between the sacred and the secular is very narrow.' An Italian Jesuit summed it up. 'I have always thought, with Ramakrishna, that we should kneel where others have kneeled, for there is the presence of God.'[2]

Certainly I was in no doubt where, so far on this pilgrimage, I had felt awe, timelessness, peace, and yes – love. The first time was in the maze on Saint Catherine's Hill, the centre emanating its own extraordinary power. Then at the Coldrum Stones, where our ancestors lie timeless on the Downs, and here, among the ruins of St Mary's Church, Eastwell. Whether this was partly due to the quiet and the loving care with which both sites are tended (who could fail to be moved by 'The Friends of Friendless Churches?') or whether by some more mysterious, elusive presence, I do not know. But I do know that in these places I found spiritual nourishment and that God is, in some very special way, there. I was in no doubt that they are sacred places and that I was standing on holy ground.

I wondered whether we would feel the next day, when we reached Becket's shrine, that we were standing on holy ground. A French woman who has made many pilgrimages wrote to me of her arrival at Santiago de Compostela:

The last miles are a harrowing assertion of your right, as a cyclist, to ride on that road, almost squeezed out of existence by thundering, articulated lorries and other such pachyderms, practically drowned by torrential downpours and muddy sprays from other road-users; then, not knowing where to go once you reach the inner city roundabouts, with buses honking behind you as you hover; and no one able to tell you where the offices of the Acogermento de Peregrinos might be, so that you can know in which direction to head for your night's rest. But once all that is over, you again melt in the collective fervour of the crowds in the huge cathedral and you are *home* ~ or as close to it as you will ever get on this earth. We then queued to place our hand on the Tree of Jesse column at the centre of the Portal of Glory ~ not a religious gesture for us, but an acknowledgement of being a link in an unbroken chain of pilgrims who, down the ages, have worn the stone smooth in the shape of a hand.[3]

This seemed to me what arriving in a holy place should be like. The harsh reality of everyday life, noisy, confusing, uncomfortable; feeling lost; not knowing where you will sleep. Then the assurance of being at home, of being just one pilgrim in a continuous stream. Would it be like that for us?

When we could bring ourselves to leave, we passed near Plantagenet's Well, so called because an unmarked tomb is believed to mark the resting place of Richard Plantagenet, bastard son of Richard III, who lived there as a humble bricklayer, and in less than half a mile we rejoined the Pilgrims' Way at Boughton Lees. Here the Way leaves its south-easterly direction and follows the contours of the Downs to the northeast ~ a natural turning that lends support to the instinct that we were indeed on the Old Road. Our next stopping place was the church at Boughton Aluph, where, I had read, the medieval pilgrims would have rested before facing the dangers of the robber-infested King's Wood. It would have been a good place to rest, for the south porch contained an unusual comfort, a fireplace; the brick chimney, thought to be unique, still survives. The church is now less hospitable, only open at weekends and on Bank Holidays, the explanation no doubt contained in a notice asking us to 'Please close door to keep out sheep'.

Time was acquiring a strange new dimension. I found it was passing not only in hours and days but in visible change. When we left Winchester (was it twelve days ago or a year and twelve days?) the bluebells were fresh and upright; here they were drooping and coming to the end of their short lives. In Hampshire the elderflower trees were innocent of flowers; now we had reached Kent they were tentatively dressed in white, wafting reminders of home-made wine. The lambs were noticeably larger, clinging less urgently to their mothers. The innocent yellow green of very early spring was darkening to the bluer green of the middle of May. Passing through time in this way was yet another reminder of how far we normally live from nature.

So too was time thrown in the melting pot as we walked in medieval footsteps, surrounded by reminders of man from Neolithic times to the twentieth century. It was a long way from living in one place, aware of the day of the week, the regular pattern of each working day. By now I was tired for much of the time and at one level longed to reach Canterbury, for the pilgrimage to be over and to be able to take my aching back to the comfort of my own home and to see my neglected garden in its spring freshness. Yet I also knew I would be heartbroken if anything were to prevent me from finishing the journey, from meeting the challenge. Indeed there was a sense in which I wanted to continue in this mode for ever, for this new apprehension of space and time to become my life.

From the church at Boughton Aluph it was a five-mile walk to Chilham. The semi-hypnotic state that had come over me at intervals was now almost continuous and my memory for the detail of the next two hours walking is shaky. I remember a beautiful stretch of rolling Kentish countryside, then passing Soakham Farm, derelict and silent apart from a few chickens, apparently left to fend for themselves. We resisted the temptation to rest in a barn full of soft comfortable hay and continued past Soakham Downs, walking for the next hour or so in a daze of content along the edge of King's Wood, imagining the bandits of medieval times, admiring the beautiful way it was managed by the Forestry Commission. We were on the summit of the Downs, some five hundred feet above sea level; the air was bracing, the day one of those fresh, light May days that Britons dream of when they are abroad in spring. We saw no one for miles.

My tiredness - and perhaps my state of mind - was beginning to affect my walking and I was constantly falling over; on one occasion I came a real purler and was amused by one of my companions, who could not restrain her delight that at last she could use the TCP, antispetic wipes and plasters that she had been gallantly carrying for over a hundred miles. After the application of first aid I remember stones underfoot suddenly giving way to soft wood chippings; a grass snake, still as a Buddha; hearing birdsong with my right ear for the first time since we left Winchester; miles of bluebells and the feeling of walking in a tunnel of young sweet chestnut trees, occasionally glimpsing the wooded acres of Godmersham Park stretching out to our left between the trees.

The sight of Godmersham Park lifted me temporarily from my trance, for this massive Palladian mansion was often visited by Jane Austen, whose brother Edward inherited it in 1797. She frequently mentions Godmersham in her letters, and scenes from *Mansfield Park* and *Pride and Prejudice* were influenced by her visits here, charmingly remembered by one of her nieces:

I remember when Aunt Jane came to us at Godmersham

she used to bring the MS of whatever novel she was writing with her, and would shut herself up with my elder sisters in one of the bedrooms to read them aloud. I and the younger ones used to hear peals of laughter through the door, and thought it very hard that we should be shut out from what was so delightful.[4]

No doubt she would have visited the local church and seen an early representation of Thomas Becket, a carved bas-relief which shows him seated, dressed in vestments and mitre. I could not imagine what Jane Austen, with her 'exquisite touch which renders ordinary commonplace things and characters interesting'[5] would make of the worldly, passionate martyr.

The Pilgrims' Way would originally have continued straight through Chilham Park, but, as at Albury, Gatton, Titsey, Chevening and most recently at Eastwell, there is no longer right of access, so we followed a lower route, staying on the North Downs Way for the last mile to Chilham. Chilham is probably one of the most beautiful villages in England, it was our last stop before Canterbury, and the last of the thirteen places where, according to Belloc, the Old Road passes right up to a ruined or existing church; we were glad that we had arrived earlier than we expected and could appreciate the village at leisure. It was after two o'clock and we did not intend to walk any farther that day, so we made ourselves at home at The White Horse, which was to be our base for the next few hours, and had an excellent lunch.

The guidebook claims that Chilham is 'a microcosm of the history of England' and the facts support the claim. Julliberrie's Barrow nearby dates from the same period as Stonehenge, suggesting that Chilham could be the earliest known settlement in this part of Kent; the castle has Roman foundations; when the Romans left, Chilham remained an Anglo-Saxon stronghold for several hundred years. Its list of distinguished residents include Lucius the Briton, Vortigern the Dane, Hengist the Jute and Withraed, the eighth-century

King of Kent; it is associated with King Canute, William the Conqueror, King John and the Peasants' Rebellion of 1450.

It is a picturesque village, winning awards for 'Best Kept Village' and much frequented by film crews and tourists. It has the antique shops, tea shops and gift shops typical of the sort of British village that is eager to attract tourists; every year there is a May Fair, Morris Dancing, a Young Men and Maidens Race around the village and a Garden Safari. Its weekly market dates back to 1260 and the Heronry from 1280.

For all that it is still a living village, clearly much loved by its residents and its history is absorbed into its bricks and stones. Its oldest symbol, an ancient yew tree, was proved to have been planted about AD 690, within 90 years of St Augustine's arrival in Canterbury and centuries before Becket was its archbishop. In fact at one time Chilham was the home of the bones of the great Saint Augustine, which were brought there in 1535, in anticipation of the plundering of the monasteries by Henry VIII. The bones are lost, but the ancient sarcophagus remains.

My wanderings round this beautiful village were cut short by the pain in my back. It was so bad that, as it was mid-afternoon and the pub was empty (though still open) I asked the friendly landlord of The White Horse if I could have the hospitality of his floor for a few minutes. He said that of course I could, and that he had the same trouble himself, so for a blissful half-hour I stretched out in a corner, once again grateful to twentieth-century hospitality to aching pilgrims.

Just as we were so indebted to the kindness of publicans, so I must pay tribute to our overnight lodgings, our modern hospices. The standard of cleanliness and kindness, the size of the breakfasts and the warmth of the welcome impressed us all along the route, but never more so than at Mannamead, a bed and breakfast house on the Pilgrims' Way near Harrietsham, where we spent our last two nights and where we returned when we had seen all we had the energy to see of Chilham. It was the attitude of Mrs Atkins, the proprietor, that particularly impressed me. 'I think of the pilgrims as mine, because we're on the Pilgrims' Way. Sometimes they turn up muddy and drowned, but I feel responsible for them.' Like the Snells at Oxted she always tried to find them somewhere to stay if she was full. 'It's what I feel I'm here for.' Her guests clearly appreciate the atmosphere she provides. She was particularly delighted by some Canadians, who stayed several nights, cooking barbecues in the garden and making themselves so much at home that when the last room was taken for a night by another guest they asked, 'Who was that person in our house?' Another group of guests wrote in the Visitors' Book 'If ever there was a Pilgrims' Rest, this is it.' We agreed with that.

It was Mrs Atkins who told us about the pub where we ate that evening. As it was our last evening together we wanted to celebrate the near-completion of our walk, so we asked her if there was somewhere special nearby, and she suggested we try The Ringlestone Inn, just up the road. It was an inspired suggestion.

The Ringlestone Inn was built in 1533, originally as a hospice for monks, but around 1615 it became one of the early 'Ale Houses'. It still has its original brick and flint walls and floors, oak beams, inglenooks and old English oak furniture. When the dining room was added the tables were specially made from the timbers of an eighteenth-century Thames barge. But what appealed to me even more was its recent history, which I had learnt from the barman at The White Horse.

Apparently for twenty years after the war it was run by two eccentric women, a mother and her daughter, whose cross-eyes held a powerful attraction for the local gallants. (Apparently it is good luck to sleep with a cross-eyed woman.) They ran the pub like a private house, wine in crystal glasses and spit-roast game served mainly to their friends, who came preferably from the forces, though it was considered better still if they were officers. The rest of the world had to knock to gain admittance and the women would admit people of whom only they approved. Even more curiously, they would only serve whatever drink they felt disposed to offer. Assuming you were allowed in, you might ask a for a half of bitter and find yourself holding a double whisky, or the other way round, depending on their whim.

All this came to the ears of a national newspaper, who sent a reporter down to do a story. As he came into the bar he found himself facing neither a pint of bitter nor a double whisky, but a twelve-bore shotgun, held by one of the women. And she used it, the shot glancing across the top of his head and only just missing him. The women then nailed up the door and the police arrived to find two hundred people trying to get in. The women seem to have escaped lightly, simply being persuaded that it was time they retired.

The fame of the pub reached some Americans, who wanted to transport it, stone by stone, to the States. I am glad they didn't, for with its medieval atmosphere, the excellent food and the best elderflower wine I have ever drunk, it was the perfect way to celebrate our last evening meal together.

CANTERBURY CATHEDRAL

Chapter Seventeen

Chilham to Canterbury
Arrival

It was a bright day and very quiet as we packed up and left Mannamead to set out on our last day's walk; even the gentle thrum of the Marley Tiles factory down the valley seemed to be only my own nervousness made audible.

I was as apprehensive as on that first day nearly a fortnight ago. We were nearly there, we had almost reached our goal. What would it be like? Would arriving at Canterbury be an anticlimax or would it bring a feeling of great achievement? Most of all I wondered whether I would find the martyred Becket's shrine a holy place or merely a tourist sight. So too the end of our pilgrimage meant the return to normal life, and I wasn't too sure what I felt about that. Almost every habit had been broken, or at least put on hold; I did not even miss doing the Independent newspaper's Concise Crossword any longer. What would it be like, leaving the liminal state that had become so comfortable?

Barbara left us at Chilham, the residents quiet behind closed doors, the shops not yet open, and we set off, going almost directly north to Old Wives Lees, under an avenue of poplar, planted as shelter for the nearby orchards. The apple blossom had fallen and the fruits were just beginning to form, though they had a long way to go before they would be picked and put in the huge boxes, stacked expectantly in a corner of the field. As we continued through hop fields, we passed what is now an unusual sight, an unconverted oast house.

There were no problems with the route, physical tiredness

became irrelevant as we approached the end, there were no fellow walkers, we did not even see any farm workers. The mind was free for fantasy, to imagine medieval voices pleading 'St Thomas, heal me', to wonder what I hoped for, then to correct anticipation by reasserting my determination to expect nothing, to take the experience moment by moment and to live in the present.

The present was about to provide something which savoured of the miraculous. We were walking through this charmed land of orchards when the skies darkened and the rain began to fall. In moments it had become a hailstorm, windy, cold and very wet. The day had started so auspiciously that we were not dressed for such a downpour, but hardly had we begun to wonder what to do, when we approached a private house and a collection of farm buildings. We gratefully took cover in a huge Dutch barn, hoping that the owners would not mind, and wondered how long we would have to wait. In ten minutes it was over. Once again the birds announced the return of fair weather and the sun shone.

What made this so extraordinary was that these were the only buildings we were to pass that morning and this ten-minute storm was the only break in the weather during the whole day – and only the second time it had rained since we left Winchester. Half thinking with medieval minds as we were, finding shelter at just this moment did indeed seem a miracle.

Soon we crossed the site of Bigbury Camp, an Iron Age settlement which, when excavated a hundred years ago, yielded iron cart-tyres, horseshoes, bits, plough coulters, sickles and adzes – cutting tools with arched blades. But little remains to be seen, in any case my mind was not in the Iron Age but in the immediate future, for we were approaching the point where we would get our first view of Canterbury Cathedral. Soon the Pilgrims' Way became a No Through Road, passing some expensive houses, and we were there. To our right the river Stour wandered in a leisurely way through fields and woods, and straight ahead, framed by large trees and topped by a sky still dark from the recent storm, was Canterbury Cathedral.

It was an amazing moment. I thought of stout Cortez, 'silent, upon a peak in Darien'; of pilgrims approaching Mecca; of our predecessors along this route, who might have stopped at just this point; of the first time I saw Chartres Cathedral across the plain of Beauce; of seeing the Delphic Charioteer, so much more than its photos had ever suggested; of the first sight of a dearly loved friend, long unseen. I thought again of Keats, standing alone and thinking, 'Till love and fame to nothingness do sink.' Even of Revelation, 'And I saw the holy city, new Jerusalem, coming down from God out of heaven, prepared as a bride adorned for her husband.'

Was this the moment of arrival? For a while it seemed to be; but just to see the object of our journey was clearly not enough, we had to be there. So at considerable risk we negotiated the A2 (it amazed me that crossing a dual carriageway and scrambling over the barrier in the middle of the very busy road was not only allowed, but seemed to be the only way), climbed Golden Hill and at last met the road taken by Chaucer's pilgrims from Southwark at Harbledown, the town Chaucer called 'Bob-up-and-down'. And there were the almshouses, built in the 1840s on the site of the leper hospital, whose floor sloped down to allow it to be washed after lepers had passed.

In the almshouses there is still a part of one of Becket's shoes, encased in brass and crystal. Erasmus and John Colet, Dean of Saint Paul's, visiting Canterbury in 1514, were apparently invited to kiss this relic. For the Dean, having already declined to accept a piece of a linen handkerchief used by Becket, this was too much. 'What, do these asses imagine we must kiss every good man's shoe?' he exclaimed. 'Why, by the same rule, they might offer his spittle or his dung to be kissed.'[1] Erasmus, in irenic mood, felt impelled to make the peace by giving a rather larger donation than he might otherwise have offered.

But an even more significant visitor to Harbledown was Henry II, and it was of him I was thinking when we went into the pub opposite the almshouses for lunch.

There is no doubt that it was Henry's remark that had triggered Becket's violent death, but there is no reason to believe that he had murder in his heart. How did he react to the news of the murder of his friend turned enemy? That he had no thought of violence is indicated by the fact that as the knights were travelling to England with murderous intent, he was summoning a council to decide what to do about the troublesome archbishop. It was decided merely that he should be arrested. All reports agree that when he heard the news Henry was distraught. He could not unsay his rash words, but he could, and did, admit that it was they that had been the cause, if unwittingly, of the archbishop's murder.

Whether his distress was fear for his reputation, especially in the face of Becket's popularity with the people, guilt at his involvement, or sadness at losing a once close friend, is hard to determine, but that it was genuine is not in question. He clothed himself in sackcloth and ashes, shut himself up for three days, eating little but milk and almonds and protesting his innocence. The Bishop of Lisieux wrote to the Pope saying that the king was so tormented that they had begun to fear for his life and beseeching him to indicate the king's innocence by punishing the perpetrators of the crime. But ironically one of the causes for which Becket stood - that laymen who murdered priests should be tried only by clerical courts - meant that his murderers could not be punished with more than excommunication. It is believed that the murderers were simply sent on pilgrimage to the Holy Land and may have died there.

It is generally thought that Henry did not make his penance until 1174, but he was not one to do things by halves; his remorse might have been slow in being publicly admitted, but it was at least wholehearted. An additional spur to penitence could have been that the King needed the martyr's support, for his kingdom was in serious trouble – his sons were rebelling against him and he was facing an invasion from Scotland. He set off from Normandy and arrived at Southampton in July 1174. Living on bread and water, he travelled, probably along the Pilgrims' Way as we had done, to Canterbury.

When he reached Harbledown he stopped at the leper-house and ordered that they be given 20 marks a year from the royal purse (still today the sum of £13.33 is paid annually by the Crown). As the cathedral came into view he dismounted and walked to the outskirts of the city. Here he took off his boots and, his bare feet bleeding as he walked over the cobbled roads, he arrived at the cathedral. In tears, he kissed the ground where Becket had fallen and went to the crypt, where he prostrated himself before the coffin. He then removed his cloak, put his head and shoulders through one of the openings in the tomb and asked for the prayers of those present and for punishment. He received five strokes of the rod from every bishop present and three from every monk. As there were eighty monks present, they must have stayed their hands, otherwise he could hardly have survived such a flagellation. Weak and bleeding, he offered £24 and a silk pall at the shrine, assigned land to the convent and promised to build a monastery in honour of Becket and to restore the rights for which the martyr had died.

Even this was not enough for the king to feel purged of his sin. He spent the whole night lying on the ground in full view of the visiting pilgrims, who he had insisted should be allowed to enter and witness their monarch's shame. The next morning he attended Mass and left, a phial of water mixed with the blood of the martyr hanging round his neck. Soon he heard that the invasion from Scotland had been quelled and that his sons were no longer able to sustain the rebellion against their father. His former friend and archbishop must have looked kindly on him, for the tide of his fortunes had turned.

Perhaps we should all have travelled the last two miles to the cathedral together, a band of pilgrims reaching our goal, but my wish to walk alone was strong, also I wanted to leave plenty of time to wander round the cathedral before Evensong at 3.30, so I asked my companions if they would mind if I set off on my own. I discovered later that one of them did, a little, but I'm afraid that selfishness won the day and I set off.

Across a roundabout, onto the London Road, past the *Pilgrim Hospice*, along Saint Dunstan's Street and into the Westgate. All the way I was in a state of such excitement and apprehension that I hardly took in my surroundings. I suppose it was fear of arrival being an anticlimax that was at the root of my nervousness, but I was filled with extravagant and absurd thoughts. I felt as if I was approaching life itself – or was it death? I remembered having the same feeling when I was walking the maze at Leeds Castle and wondered if perhaps there was a symbolic truth there somewhere, though I could not, and still cannot, see what it could be. My fears took more concrete form as I became convinced that now, at the eleventh hour, something was going to prevent me reaching the shrine – a turned ankle, a traffic accident. Fantasy went into overdrive as I imagined myself collapsing with a heart attack within yards of the cathedral; as every bus seemed about to dispatch me to the next world. Once in the Westgate I calmed down a little, the milling tourists became modern pilgrims as I sought the calm of the Eastbridge Hospital, founded in 1180 as a lodging place for poor pilgrims. Eight hundred years later and its doors were still open; I could enter freely, and spent a few moments seeing where the medieval pilgrims would have slept and worshipped.

Through the Westgate, the last surviving gate of the original eight, and I was standing before the cathedral. I half closed my eyes and imagined the scene so vividly depicted by Jonathan Sumption:

The pilgrim was greeted at his destination by a scene of raucous tumult. On the feast day of the patron saint a noisy crowd gathered in front of the church. Pilgrims mingled with jugglers and conjurers, souvenir sellers and pickpockets. Hawkers shouted their wares and rickety food stalls were surrounded by mobs of hungry travellers. Pilgrims hobbling on crutches or carried on stretchers tried to force their way through the crush at the steps of the church. Cries of panic were drowned by bursts of hysterical laughter from nearby taverns, while beggars played on horns, zithers and tambourines.[2]

This passage reminded me of the hawkers and beggars, the sick, the poor and the maimed, thronging noisily and excitedly around Indian temples, like Sri Chamundeswari near Mysore. But the confusion round the cathedral on this twentieth-century day in the middle of May had a very different cause. It was building and repair work that was causing the noise and confusion, the great West Door was covered with scaffolding and firmly closed. I had known about this, but had quite forgotten and was disappointed that my first view of the cathedral should not be the magnificent nave. I followed the signs directing visitors (and pilgrims) round the cloisters, and suddenly a new excitement gripped me. The silver lining round the cloud of frustration caused by the building work was, surely, that I would enter as Becket had on the fateful day of his martyrdom, by the northwest transept.

Becket was walking with me as I followed the directions this way and that, passing an old man being helped down the steps by a St John's Ambulance man - 'It's all right, I can manage,' the professional kept assuring an anxious woman, presumably the old man's wife. Through the cloisters and I was there, not, as I had hoped, by Saint Thomas's shrine, but in the Jesus Chapel. My disappointment that I had not been walking in Becket's footsteps soon disappeared and I lit a candle for John (I was sure Thomas would not mind my preferring my husband to him) and was about to sit down quietly for a while, when I realized that they were beginning to clear the cathedral for Evensong and I had only a short time to spend at the places in the Cathedral that are particularly associated with Becket.

First I went to the site of his martyrdom, the Altar of the Sword's Point, so named after the tip of one of the knights' swords which broke off in the fatal struggle. It is impressively simple - replicas of three swords outlined starkly against the white wall, a plain table and the word 'Thomas' inscribed on the floor. Then to the Eastern Crypt, where the body originally lay, now marked only by a stone slab, and up the flight of stone steps leading to the Trinity Chapel. Many of the pilgrims would have climbed these steps on their knees, and the undulations made by their constant passing are a vivid reminder of the devotion the saint inspired. From 1220 until Henry VIII had it demolished in 1538, they would pray before a magnificent shrine; now it is a bare space, an expanse of stone flags with a candle in the middle.

This austere space is very moving, leaving more to the imagination than an ornate reliquary, but how impressive the huge golden tomb must have been, once one of the richest shrines in the Christian world. It stood in the centre of the chapel, a gold-covered chest encrusted with jewels, supported on pink marble columns standing on a stepped plinth. A Venetian diplomat who saw it in the sixteenth century described it thus:

> Notwithstanding its great size it is entirely covered with plates of pure gold. But the gold is scarcely visible beneath a profusion of gems, including sapphires, diamonds, rubies and emeralds. Everywhere that the eye turns something even more beautiful appears. The beauty of the materials is enhanced by the astonishing skill of human hands. Exquisite designs have been carved all over it and immense gems worked delicately into the

patterns. Finest of all is a ruby, no larger than a man's thumbnail, which is set into the altar at the right hand side, and which . . . I believe, was the gift of the King (Louis VII) of France. [3]

King Louis, the first King of France to visit England, also left a gold cup - indeed so many gifts were left by the pilgrims that it took eight men to lift the chest of treasures when Henry ordered their removal. A small light in the 'Miracle Windows' depicting the miracles of healing attributed to Saint Thomas, gives some idea of how it would have looked.

I could have spent a long time looking at these glowing windows, some of the oldest and finest stained glass in the cathedral, but it was time for Evensong, so I joined my companions and relaxed as the choir sang all seventy-two verses of Psalm 78.

We had done it, we had walked a hundred and fifty miles and we were there, in Thomas's cathedral, where he worshipped and celebrated Mass, very near the place where he was murdered and the site of the shrine where so many had come to pray to him and ask for his intervention in their lives. I felt closer to him, warmer towards him. (It seemed significant that at last, like a true Becket lover, I could refer to him as 'Thomas'.) Somehow he was present as a brave and stubborn man, standing up for his beliefs, and I could admire him, even love him, for his courage and doggedness. But could I revere him as a saint? At that moment it did not seem important. I felt a deep peace - not to mention considerable physical relief that the long days of walking were over - and a small sense of achievement. But my mind had slipped into neutral, overwhelmed by the significance that was there, somewhere, but unable to pull coherent thoughts out of the maze of emotions. The confluence of past and present, of the inner and the outer journeys, had met in this place, in this moment, and I could only sit, overwhelmed by the beauty that surrounded me.

The ancient beauty of the cathedral, the timeless chanting of the psalm, took me beyond thought. I could identify now with Richard Church, visiting the cathedral in the 1940s.

My immediate desire, when I first saw the massive but featherweight pillars receding in perspective up the aisle, with their fellows along the nave crowding together through the angle from which I saw them, was to lift my arms likewise, and to seek a high place to add to my endeavour. I wanted to shout with the voice of an army of men entering somewhere in triumph. But of course I stood there, doltlike and dumb . . . I can see myself standing there, hat in hand, with an agonized attention flickering away from the superb spectacle before and above me, flickering away to read the tickets on the collection-boxes and the booklets inside the door, then coming hopelessly back to that grandeur again, and once more failing.[4]

So I too sat 'doltlike and dumb', until the psalm at last ended and Canon Christopher Lewis introduced the lesson by saying that 'Moses is telling the people of Israel that when they arrive in the Promised Land, they must not forget to be grateful to God and generous to others'. It did not matter that I had no great thoughts. For the moment gratitude was enough.

After Evensong we crossed the cathedral square to one of the elegant houses that surround the cathedral. Christopher and Rhona Lewis, whom I had known for some years, welcomed us most royally, toasting us in champagne and offering us tea, sandwiches, cakes and the warmest hospitality. They had also invited Canon Derek Ingram Hill and his wife. The Canon knows more about the cathedral than any living soul (he wrote his first guidebook when he was eleven), so he was well able to answer our questions.

Eventually we left and drove back to Oxford. For much of

the early part of the journey the road runs parallel with the Pilgrims' Way. It felt very odd, speeding in the opposite direction, past the places that we had known so recently and explored at such a leisurely pace. The journey that had taken us nearly fourteen days to walk was over in less than three hours. Then home to a pile of post and messages and a broken washing machine. Life must now return to normal, but would it ever be quite the same again?

FISH AND ANCHOR — EARLY SYMBOLS OF FAITH

Epilogue

The pilgrimage is over. We are back in our various homes, picking up the strands of day-to-day life – at one level very much like returning after a holiday, though unlike a holiday, which can be wiped from the mind within days, the memory of this fortnight was to stay with me for months, perhaps much longer, for writing less than a year later I cannot yet know.

But if I had been worried by the significance of that first step from Winchester, it was nothing compared to my concern with when, exactly, the pilgrimage had ended. Was it that luminous moment when we first saw Canterbury Cathedral from the top of the hill, dominating the surrounding countryside? Or when I reached the Eastbridge Hospital, a resting place for thousands of pilgrims? Or the moment when I stood in the cathedral precincts, barred from entering through the great West Door?

We had set out to reach the shrine of Thomas Becket, so the end should have been at one of the places associated with his martyrdom, but it had not seemed so. Nor did I have a feeling of finality as we heard Evensong, drank champagne with the Lewises, or even as I put my key in my own front door.

It was not until the next morning, when I went to Mass at Oxford's Benedictine College, Saint Benet's, that I had any sense of completion. Only then did I begin to realize how I had been changed. On the physical level, fitter than I had been for years, I was relaxed and comfortable in my body, able to stay still more easily than usual; in that way I had, I suppose, found a healing I had not consciously sought. Mentally I was more centred, less open to distractions, spiritually involved in the drama of the Masss as never before. The hours of trying, consciously, to live in the present had left their mark and I felt totally in the present moment, totally in that particular place - a conjunction of time and place that gave a new significance to the centre of the crucifix. There is no duality, not between dark and light, or God and Man, or journey and arrival. All is one.

In the homily the priest spoke of the gospels giving us a paradigm, but that we each had to find our own way. This was eerily in tune with my mood. I was very conscious that there were many aspects of pilgrimage - saints, relics, shrines, for instance - that I had not been able to relate to as fully as the medieval pilgrims would all have done and as some Christians still do. Aware too that the places I had found most holy were not the traditionally sacred centres of Christendom. Though concerned with our arrival and with its symbolic parallel, the soul's destination, it was the journey itself that was the point. It was as the priest said: we had, each of us, both walked the same path and found our own individual ways.

I had been changed by this pilgrimage, but I do not expect to know how for a long time. Though on this Sunday morning I knew the pilgrimage had reached some sort of completion, it had not ended. This symbolic microcosm of the inner journey had to find its resonances with the longer, day-to-day, pilgrimage. Perhaps my inability to know when it ended was a precise reflection of its inner parallel. We were resuming our day-to-day lives, our journeys of perpetual pilgrimage. This pilgrimage from Winchester to Canterbury had not ended on arrival any more than life ends with death. But I did feel that I understood a little better where the sacred place is to be found.

March 1994

References

Chapter One

1 *The Oxford Dictionary of the Christian Church*, Ed. F. L. Cross, Oxford University Press, 1983
2 *The Tablet*, 6 March, 1993
3 Ralegh, Walter, *His Pilgrimage*, *Oxford Book of English Verse*, Clarendon Press, 1907
4 *Pilgrimage – An image of mediaeval religion*, Jonathan Sumption, Faber and Faber, 1975, p. 300
5 Ibid., p. 182
6 Quoted in *God of a hundred names*, Barbara Greene and Victor Gollanz, Trafalgar, 1985

Chapter Two

1 Quoted in *The Pilgrims' Way from Winchester to Canterbury*, Sean Jennett, Cassell, 1971, p. 79
2 Alan Charles, *Exploring the Pilgrims' Way – Winchester to Canterbury*, Countryside Books, 1990
3 Hilaire Belloc, *The Old Road*, Constable, 1911, p. 126
4 *The I Ching* or Book of Changes, The Richard Wilhelm translation rendered into English by Cary F. Baynes, Routledge and Kegan Paul, 1951, p. 115
5 Edward Thomas, *The South Country*, Tuttle, 1993

Chapter Three

1 Belloc, op. cit., p. 14
2 Gilbert White, *Naturalist's Journal*, Century Hutchinson, 1989
3 Arnold van Gennep, *The Rites of Passage*, University of Chicago Press, 1961
4 Victor Turner, *Image and Pilgrimage in Christian Culture*, Columbia University Press, 1978, p. 249
5 Sumption, op. cit., p. 101
6 Aldous Huxley, *Brave New World*, HarperCollins, 1989

Chapter Four

1 Belloc, op. cit., p. 4
2 Ibid., p. 92
3 Ibid., p. 93
4 Ibid., p. 89
5 Ibid., p. 11

Chapter Five

1 *The Cloud of Unknowing*, Viking-Penguin, 1978, p. 60
2 Thomas à Kempis, *The Imitation of Christ*, Viking-Penguin, 1952, p. 173
3 Gwen Ware, *The White Monks of Waverly*, Farnham and District Museum Society, 1976
4 Merton, T., *Seeds of Contemplation*, New Directions, 1986
5 William Cobbett, *Rural Rides*, Penguin Classics, 1985, p. 153
6 Lao Tzu, *Tao Te Ching*, tr. Gia-Fu Feng and Jane English, Random House, 1989
7 Ibid., No. 47

Chapter Six

1 Tully, M., *No full stops in India*, Penguin, 1991, p. 123
2 Gregory of Nyssa, *On Pilgrimage*, in Schaff, P. and Wace, H. (eds) *The Nicene and Post-Nicene Fathers*, Michigan, 1892, 2nd series, Vol. 5, pp. 382-3. Quoted in *Theology*, September 1989

3 William Langland, *Piers the Ploughman*, tr. J. G. Goodridge, Viking-Penguin, 1959
4 Sumption, op. cit., pp. 93-4
5 Ian Reader and Tony Walter, *Pilgrimage in Popular Culture*, Macmillan Press, 1993, p. 226
6 Ibid., p. 79

Chapter Seven

1 Walter Hilton, *The Ladder of Perfection*, Viking-Penguin, 1988
2 K. H. Jackson, *A Celtic Miscellany*, p. 136, Viking-Penguin, 1972
3 Quoted in *On going to Sacred Places*, Christopher Lewis, *Theology*, September 1989
4 Thomas à Kempis, op. cit., p. 580
5 Hughes, G., *The Tablet*, March 9th, 1991
6 Quoted in Henry Fearon, *The Pilgrimage to Canterbury*, Associated Newspapers
7 Ibid., p. 14
8 Nigel Pennick, *Mazes and Labyrinths*, Robert Hale, 1990, p. 47
9 Bruce Chatwin, *The Songlines*, Viking-Penguin, 1988
10 David Lodge, *Paradise News*, Viking-Penguin, 1993, pp. 75-6
11 Quoted in *Pilgrimage in Popular Culture*, op. cit.

Chapter Eight

1 Quoted in *Caerdroia*, 1990, p. 15
2 de Mello, A., *Awareness*, Doubleday, 1990, p. 22
3 Cobbett, William, op. cit., p. 97

Chapter Nine

1 Eade, J. and Sallnow, J., *Contesting the Sacred; the anthropology of Christian pilgrimage*, Routledge, 1991
2 Merton, T., op. cit.
3 Sean Jennett, op. cit., p. 3
4 Ibid., p. 162
5 *The Times*, September 11th, 1967

Chapter Ten

1 *The Observer*, January 31st, 1993. Quoted from *Freya Stark – A Biography* by Molly Izzard
2 Thomas à Kempis, op. cit., p. 186

Chapter Eleven

1 Elizabeth Barrett Browning, From *Aurora Leigh*, Bk vii
2 Chaucer, *The Canterbury Tales*, Tr. Nevill Coghill, Viking Children's Books, 1951, p. 19
3 William Langland, op. cit., p. 77
4 Richard Church, *Kent*, Robert Hale, 1948, pp. 3-4
5 Shirley Toulson, *The Celtic Year*, Element Books, 1993, p. 118
6 Quoted in *Prayers for Pilgrims*, Pawley, M., Triangle, SPCK, 1991, p. 19 (Author's italics.)
7 Ibid., p. 128
8 Church, op. cit., p. 56
9 Church, op. cit., p. 57
10 Quoted in Church, op. cit., p. 54

Chapter Twelve

1 Frank Barlow, *Thomas Becket*, University of California Press, 1990, pp. 24-5
2 Ibid., p. 47
3 *Dictionary of Saints*, Penguin, 1965
4 Barlow, op. cit., p. 100
5 Ibid., p. 235
6 Ibid., p. 250
7 Ibid., p. 274
8 Benedicta Ward, *Miracles and the Medieval Mind*, University of Pennsylvania Press, 1982, p. 189

Chapter Thirteen

1 *The Oxford Dictionary of the Christian Church*, op. cit., p. 1234 (Author's italics.)
2 Jacquetta Hawkes, *A guide to the Prehistoric and Roman Monuments in England and Wales*, Chatto and Windus, 1951, p. 49

Chapter Fourteen

1 Hawkes, op. cit., p. 69
2 Hawkes, loc. cit.
3 Church, op. cit., p. 251
4 Sumption, op. cit., p. 198
5 Ibid., pp. 201-2
6 Chaucer, op. cit., p. 39
7 Sumption, op. cit., p. 203

Chapter Fifteen

1 Church, op. cit., p. 255
2 Ware, T., *The Orthodox Church*, Viking-Penguin, 1963
3 Quoted in Sumption, op. cit., p. 23
4 Ward, op. cit., p. 57
5 Sumption, op. cit., p. 82

Chapter Sixteen

1 T. S. Eliot, op. cit.
2 Quoted in *To Lhasa and beyond*, Giuseppe Tucci, Snow Lion Publications, 1988
3 Letter to author from Jeanne Gandrey de Quercize
4 Quoted in *Jane Austen and Godmersham*, The Rev S. Graham Brade-Birks, Kent County Council
5 Sir Walter Scott, *Quarterly Review*, 1815

Chapter Seventeen

1 Quoted in *The Pilgrims' Way – Shrines and Saints in Britain and Ireland*, Blair, J., Book Club Association, 1978, p. 71
2 Sumption, op. cit., p. 211
3 Ibid., p. 155
4 Church, op. cit., p. 282

Other Books Consulted

Ady, J., *The Pilgrims' Way*, AMS Press (reprint of 1893 edition)

Anouilh, Jean, *Becket*, Berkley, 1960

Barber, R., *Pilgrimages*, Boydell and Brewer, 1991

Belloc, Hailaire, *The Path to Rome*, Regnery, 1987

Bryant, Arthur, *The Story of England – Makers of the Realm*, Collins, 1953

Clanchy, M. T., *England and its rulers*, Fontana, 1989

Eliade, M., *The Sacred and the Profane*, Peter Smith, 1983

Eliot, T. S., *Murder in the Cathedral*, Harcourt Brace, 1964

Finucane, R. A., *Miracles and Pilgrims: Popular Beliefs in Medieval England*, Dent, 1977

Hall, D. J., *English Mediaeval Pilgrimage*, Routledge and Kegan Paul, 1965

Harper-Bill, C., *Thomas Becket*, Cathedral Gifts

Heath, S., *In the Steps of the Pilgrims*, Rich and Cowan, 1950

Jackson, B., *Places of Pilgrimage*, Geoffrey Chapman, 1989

Keen, M., *English Society in the Later Middle Ages 1348-1500*, Viking-Penguin, 1991

Maxwell, Donald, *The Pilgrims' Way in Kent*, Kent Messenger

Mayr-Harting, H., *The Miracles of St Frideswide*, From Studies in Medieval History presented to R. H. C. Davis, ed. H. Mayr-Harting and R. I. Moore, London, 1985

McCall, A., *The Medieval Underworld*, Marboro Books, 1992

Mee, A., *The King's England. Surrey*, 1938

Morton, H. V., *In Search of England*, Methuen, 1927

Nicolson, Adam, *The National Trust Book of Long Walks*, Weidenfeld and Nicolson, 1981

Snowden-Ward, H., *The Canterbury Pilgrimage*, A. & C. Black, 1904

Southern, R. W., *Western Society and the Church in the Middle Ages*, Viking-Penguin, 1970

Turner, V., *The Ritual Process*, Cornell University Press, 1977

– *The Age of Bede*, Penguin Classics. Tr. Webb, J. F., 1965

The Way of a Pilgrim. Tr. from the Russian R. M. French, SPCK, 1965

Index

Note: The arrangement of this index is letter by letter. When a saint's name refers to the person, it is found under the initial letter of the Christian name. When it refers to a place or a building, it is found under 'S', Saint, followed by the Christian name in alphabetical order.

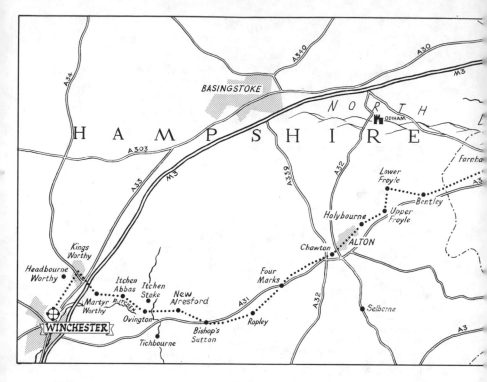

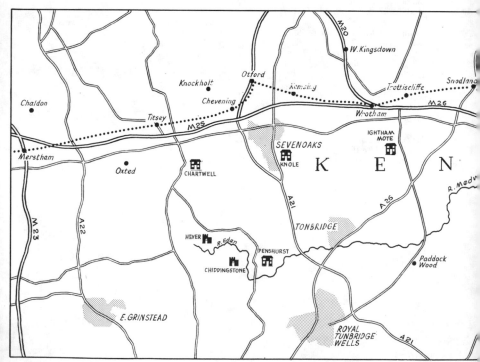